Adventures in
Booga Booga Land

Adventures in
BOOGABOOGA
LAND

The Adventures of
Marty the Monkey
and
Gerard the Giraffe

The Parables of Jesus for All Ages

RICHARD MILNER

Tommy
NELSON

A Division of Thomas Nelson Publishers

NASHVILLE   DALLAS   MEXICO CITY   RIO DE JANEIRO

Adventures in Booga Booga Land: The Adventures of Marty the Monkey and Gerard the Giraffe

© 2004, 2010 David Milner

Previously published by ACW Press.

Printed in Nashville, Tennessee, by Tommy Nelson. Tommy Nelson is a registered trademark of Thomas Nelson, Inc.

Scripture quotations taken from the Holy Bible, New International Version®, NIV®. © 1973, 1978, 1984 by Biblica, Inc.™ Used by permission of Zondervan. All rights reserved worldwide. www.zondervan.com.

ISBN: 978-1-4003-8061-9

Library of Congress Cataloging-in-Publication Data has been applied for.

Mfr: RR Donnelley/Crawfordsville, IN/August 2010/PPO# 110577

Dedicated to

the legacy of Richard Milner, which lives on

in the hearts of many . . .

May you catch a glimpse of his enthusiasm for the life

God gave him and took when it was time.

Contents

Preface

The circumstances leading to the ultimate publication of *Adventures in Booga Booga Land* turned out to be much different than originally intended, as Richard left this earth to be with his dearly loved heavenly Father before he had a chance to see his finished work in published form.

Throughout his life Richard Daniel Milner developed an extreme love for the outdoor world, which God created, superseded only by an intense love for the Creator of the universe Himself. Richard lived a life just short of forty-four years, in which he experienced more thrill and excitement and accomplished more for God than most people do in a life of eighty years. His adventures outside of his work as a mechanical engineer included competitive road-bike racing followed by a love for mountain biking. Throughout his life he loved hiking and climbing mountains and spent much time feeling close to God while exploring many on and off trail areas, especially in the Canadian Rocky Mountains.

Richard had a unique way of encouraging those he knew to seek their sense of adventure here on earth and also to go for the gusto in their service for God. Richard was a dedicated junior-high youth leader and Sunday school teacher for about fifteen years. He inspired many youth to develop an early grounding in their Christian lives and encouraged and inspired them to develop servant hearts for their Lord, for which many of them are eternally grateful. He also led services at an inner-city mission, year after year, showing love to those many saw as unlovable. Richard was one who saw past the surface condition of a person's life and was concerned with the eternal destination of their soul.

From Richard's extreme love for life itself and a love for the One who gave life to all, Richard started the project *Adventures in Booga Booga Land* several years before his passing from this earth and completed the manuscript in early 2003. He wanted to give a gift to offer continual encouragement to those who are living a life of love for their heavenly Father and to remind those who have not yet straightened their lives out with God that they need to do so while they still have time prior to their departure from this earth.

Richard's final adventure here on earth was spent doing what he loved so much—hiking in God's creation. On July 29, 2003, Richard began hiking on the Price Creek Trail headed for Cream Lake, considered by many to be the jewel of Strathcona Park on Vancouver Island, British Columbia, Canada. What exactly happened on Richard's last earthly adventure may never be known, as extensive searching by air and land has not revealed any clue of his demise. While many people thought that Richard was by himself while hiking, he would often remind people that he was never alone. God was always with him.

As was expressed at a celebration of life service for Richard on September 5, 2003, many people who were intensely inspired and encouraged by his life here on earth are left grieving. Those who personally know the Savior whom Richard loved have a deep peace that while he was headed for a small lake considered a jewel here on earth, he is now experiencing a new and wonderful adventure in heaven wearing his jeweled crown prepared for him by his heavenly Father.

While no one here on earth is certain what exactly happened to Richard during the last few moments or days of his life, one thing is known—one of Richard's characteristics that set him apart was his extreme, explosive attitude of thankfulness to God. He at one time said he was so thankful to God that he thought his thankfulness might cause him to explode to pieces, in which case he hoped that if there was only one piece of him found, it would be his thankful heart. While no bones have been found, it is certain that God has scooped up Richard's thankful heart, and many of those who knew Richard are left with a huge smile on their faces when they think of his thankful heart. They know that even if Richard spent his last few days on earth starving and thirsting to death, he would have been thanking God for the opportunity to hike this trail as his last earthly adventure.

Richard was one who lived by the principle that God has many doors to open for those who follow Him and one need not bang their head against doors that are closed when there are others wide open. So it is no surprise that when God opened the door to heaven during Richard's adventure toward Cream Lake, he took the opportunity to enter. His race is finished and he is now in the presence of God Himself.

Along the way Richard left *Adventures in Booga Booga Land* as a gift to be enjoyed. It was his desire that it be used to strengthen and expand God's kingdom, and to touch the hearts and lives of all who read it. Many of the characters in the book are extensions of Richard's character itself. Some of the experiences of Marty and Gerard came to be written directly from some of Richard's own life experiences, while others are extensions of his desires he would have liked to have experienced if he were given the opportunity.

As you read *Adventures in Booga Booga Land,* may you be inspired, challenged, and prepared for your final adventure in life wherever and whenever that may be. While Richard's days of romping around this earth are over, as wonderful as they were, he has now entered into a bigger and better adventure, and what's more, it's an adventure that will last forever. May this book help you prepare to meet Jesus face-to-face in a joyful and glorious fashion, as my brother Richard did.

David Milner

Introduction

This is a zany book. You'll find zany characters and situations, but mostly you'll be reading about a zany monkey named Marty and his zany giraffe friend, Gerard.

The best thing about Marty and Gerard is that they are best of friends. In their adventures, which change as quickly and as colorfully as a droplet falling through a rainbow, you'll be introduced to two high-spirited characters that have a bent toward living life on the edge.

The stories of Marty and Gerard are based on the parables of Jesus. Each chapter follows the story line of one parable and ends with the biblical text of that parable, as well as a comment tying story and Scripture together. I hope you will find this book an enjoyable and useful tool in bringing the teachings of Jesus to life in a new and refreshing way.

ONE
So . . . This Is Booga

Far across the ocean, close to where the sun rises, lies a mysterious land. It is a land filled with lofty mountains, rolling hills, sandy beaches, and flowery meadows. This is Booga Booga Land. At a glance it appears to be a normal land. It has people, towns and cities, cats, dogs, and farms. But Booga Booga Land is far from normal, for in it live two extraordinary characters, Marty the monkey and Gerard the giraffe. This is a story of their adventures.

There is a little town nestled in the hills of Booga Booga Land that is set so perfectly, it looks like a jewel in a king's crown. This town is called Toosmallforme, and it's the place where Gerard grew up. It's a lovely little town, and Gerard found it to be a comfortable place to live—that is, until he grew to be eighteen feet tall. It was then he noticed something very odd. Everything seemed to be small. When he tried to get into a car, it was too small. When he tried to walk into a store, he couldn't fit through the door. When he jumped into the swimming pool, the water only came up to his knees. So it really didn't come as a big surprise when one day Gerard announced he was going to leave town and travel to Booga, the capital of Booga Booga Land.

On the day Gerard's bus pulled into town, everyone showed up. No one had ever seen a giraffe get on a bus before, and most people were curious. "I'll see a snowman walk through this town before I see a giraffe get on a bus," one of the bystanders said.

Everyone around him seemed to agree.

When the driver got out of his bus, he looked at Gerard, then looked at the bus, then looked at Gerard again. "I don't think so," he said slowly. "I don't think you're going to be able to get on this bus, Mr. Giraffe."

"I'm sure I can," Gerard insisted. "Just give me a chance, please?" Gerard continued to plead with the driver, until finally he agreed to let Gerard try.

Well, at least he's giving me a chance, Gerard thought. He looked around, then grabbed his suitcase and backed up fifty paces. He then began running toward the bus. Twenty paces away, he planted his feet and jumped. Everyone held their breath as the lanky giraffe soared through the air. *I think I'm going to make it*, Gerard thought. Unfortunately, he flew over the top, and landed with a THUNK! on the other side. "Ooookay, so much for my practice run. Now, for the real thing." For his second attempt, Gerard shortened his approach, and this time he landed perfectly, right on top of the bus.

"Phew!" Gerard sighed, as he looked down at the startled driver. "I told you I could get on the bus."

A few minutes later, the bus pulled out of Toosmallforme, and Gerard was on his way to Booga.

The trip was longer than Gerard had expected, and he soon became restless. He poked his head over the side of the bus and into the driver's window. "How much further?" he asked.

"Oh, about eighty miles, give or take how far a cow can kick a can in the wind," the driver replied.

I sure hope cows can't kick cans far, Gerard thought as he paced back and forth, wondering how he would survive the long trip.

He started hunting for a newspaper, and after poking his head into several windows, he finally spotted one. As he reached over the passengers to get it, he politely said, "Excuse me. 'Scuse me. 'Scooose me." He picked up the paper with his mouth, then said, "Hank hoo. Hank hoo. Hank hoo," as he pulled his head back outside.

Reading the paper on top of the bus proved to be quite difficult, as the wind was blowing it to shreds, so he walked to the front of the bus and put it on the windshield, right in front of the driver.

This worked fine, but the driver couldn't see, and the bus began swerving from lane to lane. When the bus finally arrived in Booga, the passengers seemed to be quite sick. Gerard, on the other hand, was feeling great. He jumped off of the bus, flung his suitcase onto his back, then looked around at the big city. "So . . . this is Booga."

Gerard had managed to save only one section of the newspaper, and fortunately for him, it was the career section. He sat down on a park bench and began reading. Just then his ears picked up a faint sound. It was the wavering voice of someone in distress. The sound was coming from the sky, and it was getting louder. Gerard looked up and was surprised to see a little monkey, tumbling through the air. "Catch meeeee . . ." the little monkey cried helplessly, as he cannonballed from the sky.

"I've got you, little fella!" Gerard called out as he dropped his newspaper, then stuck out his front hooves. THUD! The monkey went right through and hit the ground. Gerard helped the little monkey to his feet.

"Are you all right?"

"I think so," the little monkey replied as he brushed himself off. "I guess mom was right when she told me not to play with airplane exit doors. Thanks for trying to catch me, though. My name's Marty. What's yours?"

"I'm Gerard."

As Marty and Gerard talked, they discovered they had a lot in common, and they quickly became friends. They decided to team up while they were in Booga and see if they could find a job together.

Marty noticed the newspaper Gerard had been reading, and he picked it up. "Here's a job for air-traffic controllers, Gerard. I think we'd be good at that!" Gerard agreed it would be worth a try, so they went to the Booga airport to inquire.

When they arrived, they walked over to the control tower, and Marty climbed onto Gerard's head. After knocking on the window, Marty heard someone inside say, "Hey Lester, we've got a monkey and a giraffe on runway number one. What should I do?"

3

"Roger, runway number one is open. They're clear for takeoff."

Roger came over to the window and opened it. "I've been instructed to tell you guys to take off."

"Roger, we're not flying anywhere," Marty gasped, taken aback by Roger's misunderstanding. "We just want to be air-traffic controllers. Do you think we could be hired on to protect your tower from low-flying aircraft?"

Just then a low-flying jet headed toward them. "Duck, Gerard!" Marty shouted. Gerard ducked and the plane zoomed over their heads. Unfortunately, it grazed the control tower, and the tower toppled over.

"Oookay, I guess not," Marty commented, as he and Gerard helped Roger and Lester push the tower back up.

"Got any other ideas, Marty?" Gerard asked as they began walking back to Booga.

Marty pulled out the paper and began scanning the career section again. "Well, Gerard, here's a job for—"

"Marty, look out!" Gerard shouted, but too late. SMACK! Marty banged into a pole, face first. He lay sprawled on the ground with his arms and legs pointing in the four directions of the compass. A moment later he got up and rubbed his nose.

"Gerard, I think my nose just got flattened."

Gerard came over and took a closer look. "Hmm, you know, Marty, it looks just as flat now as it did before."

Marty rubbed his nose again. Maybe his nose always was flat. He picked up the newspaper and showed Gerard the ad he had spotted. The job listing was for window washers. They discussed the matter, and the next day they went to the window-washing company to inquire.

When they arrived, Marty knocked on the door. They were greeted by an old man, and beside him stood a shaggy dog. "Hi, my name is Stan," the old man said, "and this here's my dog, Rufus."

While Stan and Gerard talked about the window-washing job, Marty found a stick and went to play with Rufus. "Here, boy, go fetch!" Marty pretended to throw the stick, then hid it behind his back. Rufus bounded after the stick, then stopped with a bewildered look on his face.

Just then Gerard called out, "Hey, Marty, Stan agreed to hire us. We're going to get twenty bamolies!"

Woah! Marty thought. *Twenty bamolies! That'll sure buy a lot of bananas.* Marty started walking back to Stan and Gerard, as Rufus rubbed his head, still wondering what Marty had done with that stick.

The next morning, just as the sun was rising, Marty and Gerard went to the job site to begin work. Marty took a pail of water and the window squeegee, then climbed onto Gerard's head.

As Marty held the squeegee, Gerard nodded his head up and down. "This is fun, huh Gerard?" Marty said, as the tiring giraffe just kept on nodding. After working for three hours, they were surprised to see another window washer show up.

"How many bamolies are you getting?" Marty asked curiously.

"Don't know. Stan just said he'd pay me whatever seemed right."

"We're getting twenty bamolies," Marty said proudly.

At lunch time, another window washer came, and a few hours later, still another.

"Marty, I wonder if Stan is throwing us a hint. Maybe he thinks we're not working hard enough. Let's pick up the pace."

At five o'clock, one hour before quitting time, another window washer came.

"Faster, Marty, faster! Only one hour to go!"

When six o'clock finally came, Marty and Gerard were exhausted— well, at least Gerard was. "Next time let's just use a fire hose, okay, Marty?" Gerard said as he rubbed his sore neck.

Stan soon arrived at the job site and the workers huddled around him to receive their paychecks. "Fine job," Stan said as he started handing out the pay envelopes.

The first worker to receive his envelope was the five o'clock worker. Marty walked over and took a peek at the check. It was for twenty bamolies.

"Gerard!" Marty whispered loudly. "This guy got twenty bamolies for one hour! We're gonna be rich!"

When Marty received his envelope, he put the butter on the popcorn: "Stan, you're the most gracious, generous, benevolent man in all of Booga. You're simply the best!"

Marty walked over to Gerard and opened the envelope.

"Stan's a cheapskate!" Marty squawked. The check was for twenty bamolies.

"Maybe he made a mistake," Gerard said. "I'll go ask."

Diplomatically, Gerard began explaining to Stan. "Uh, Stan, we noticed this check is a few peas short of a full pod. The guy who worked an hour got twenty bamolies, and well, quite frankly, we worked hard all day and only got twenty. We thought maybe you made a mistake."

"No mistake," Stan said. "You agreed to twenty bamolies, didn't you?"

"Well yeah, but—"

"And how many did you get?" Gerard walked back to Marty.

"Well, what did he say, Gerard?"

"He said we agreed to twenty bamolies."

Marty and Gerard soon realized Stan was right. They took the twenty, bought two jumbo coconut cream pies, then went for a picnic in Booga park. The pie was a perfect closer to their day, and after they'd finished eating, they smiled contentedly. It had been one long day, and the two weary window washers now found themselves nodding off. Soon the only sounds heard were the soft snores of the little monkey and the big giraffe, as Marty and Gerard serenely drifted off to Snooza Snooza Land.

The Parable of the Workers in the Vineyard

(Matthew 20:1-16)

For the kingdom of heaven is like a landowner who went out early in the morning to hire men to work in his vineyard. He agreed to pay them a denarius for the day and sent them into his vineyard.

About the third hour he went out and saw others standing in the marketplace doing nothing. He told them, "You also go and work in my vineyard, and I will pay you whatever is right." So they went.

He went out again about the sixth hour and the ninth hour and did the same thing. About the eleventh hour he went out and found still others standing around.

He asked them, "Why have you been standing here all day long doing nothing?"

"Because no one has hired us," they answered.

He said to them, "You also go and work in my vineyard."

When evening came, the owner of the vineyard said to his foreman, "Call the workers and pay them their wages, beginning with the last ones hired and going on to the first."

The workers who were hired about the eleventh hour came and each received a denarius. So when those came who were hired first, they expected to receive more. But each one of them also received a denarius. When they received it, they began to grumble against the landowner.

"These men who were hired last worked only one hour," they said, "and you have made them equal to us who have borne the burden of the work and the heat of the day."

But he answered one of them, "Friend, I am not being unfair to you. Didn't you agree to work for a denarius? Take your pay and go. I want to give the man who was hired last the same as I gave you. Don't I have the right to do what I want with my own money? Or are you envious because I am generous?"

So the last will be first, and the first will be last.

In this parable Jesus speaks of a man just like Stan, but instead of hiring window washers, this man hired men to work in his vineyard. All of these workers were hired at different times of the day, but they were all paid the same—no matter how much or how little they worked. And just like Marty and Gerard, the ones who were hired first and worked the hardest complained when they got paid, thinking they deserved more pay than the other workers. The workers in this parable represent followers of Jesus, and the parable is saying that God gives the same gift of eternal life to everyone who turns to Him, whether they turn to Him on their deathbed or whether they turn to Him early in life. Some people may think that God is being overly generous to those who turn to Him late in life, and, consequently, they may grumble. But we shouldn't grumble at the way God does things. In His kingdom He has a certain way of doing things, and His ways are often different than our ways. So even when we don't understand God's ways, just remember that He is in control—and whatever He does will always be just, right, and fair.

TWO
Marty's Sandcastle

The sun was beating down on Marty and Gerard as they walked up and down the streets of Booga, looking for jobs. Marty ran his finger through the small want-ad section of the newspaper, carefully reading each ad, as he swaggered down the sidewalk. He wasn't paying attention to where he was going and people were jumping out of the way to avoid running into the little monkey. There wasn't much of a job selection, and Marty shook his head as he—THWACK!—ran into a parking meter. He lay on the ground for a moment, looking like wet spaghetti on a plate. When he came to, he rubbed his nose, then looked up at Gerard. Gerard's attention was focused on an ice cream truck down the road, and he hadn't noticed the incident.

"Hellooo," the little monkey called out to his tall giraffe friend. Gerard looked down at Marty. "Sorry, Marty, did you say something?"

"Gerard, I think I'm going to have to install telephone lines to your head. Look, there's a bent parking meter down here, not to mention a monkey with a sore nose." Gerard looked at the parking meter. It was bent all right. He then looked at Marty's nose. It was bent too.

"I have an idea," Marty said as he did some repairs to his nose.

"I know. You think Booga should install rubber parking meters, right?"

"No, Gerard. I was thinking we should go into carpentry."

Gerard thought about the idea, then shook his head. "I don't know, Marty. Letting you work with tools sounds kind of risky. Isn't there something else we could try, something that's just a bit safer?"

"I don't think so," Marty said as he looked up at Gerard.

Gerard somehow knew Marty was right. He had a hunch that anything Marty tried would be unsafe. "Okay, Marty. We'll give it a try." The next day they went down to the Booga School of Carpentry, and enrolled.

During their first class, they listened intently to the instructor as he began explaining the course outline. "The first thing we are going to do is cover some basic safety rules, then we will move on to the use of hand tools, including the saw, the hammer . . ."

As the instructor continued talking, an electric table saw began to hum in the background. Then—ZWING! TWANG! CLANK!—pieces of wood began flying all over the classroom. Marty was using the table saw. The instructor frantically rushed over and turned the machine off.

"What are you doing?!" he exclaimed.

"You said we were going to learn how to use the saw," Marty said.

"I said the HAND saw, not the ELECTRIC saw!" the instructor said as he took Marty by the ear then escorted him back to the classroom. The instructor continued: "After we learn to use the HAND saw, the hammer, and the square . . ."

"The square?" Marty blurted out. "I know where to find one of those. There's one standing right in front of the classroom."

The teacher looked at Marty, then pointed to the floor. Marty knew what that meant, and after finishing his one hundredth push-up, he dragged himself back to his desk and sat quietly. He had gotten himself into enough trouble for one day.

After one week of sitting in the classroom, the students were finally ready to begin hands-on training. The instructor stood in front of the class and announced, "Today we are going to learn how to pound nails. Gerard, I'll start with you." Gerard picked up a hammer and a nail, and then with one mighty thwack, he pounded the nail right through a thick piece of wood.

"Very good. Okay, Marty, now it's your turn."

Marty took the nail and held it steadily with one hand, while with the other he quickly raised the hammer. Unfortunately, the hammer slipped out of his hand, flew into the air, and landed on the instructor's head. *Uh oh*, Marty thought, *this is not good.*

When the instructor returned from the hospital (several days later), Marty was given a set of rubber hand tools. *Oookay*, Marty thought as he looked at his rubber hand saw, *I guess the only thing I'll be cutting now is cookie dough.*

After two months of working with hand tools, the class was finally ready to move on to the use of power tools. The instructor began by saying, "The first piece of equipment we will be working with is the drill press."

Marty grabbed a piece of wood. Then he quickly ran over to the press.

"Marty . . ." the instructor began, but too late. The wood got jammed in the press and hit Marty on the head.

"Marty, please wait for instructions before using the equipment," the instructor said as Marty woozily picked himself up off the floor. "Instead of the drill press," the instructor continued, "maybe we should start with the circular saw." Marty ran over to the saw and picked it up, ready to squeeze the trigger. "Marty!" the instructor screamed.

"It's okay, Mr. Instructor. I've used these things before." Marty picked up a piece of wood, but didn't notice that it was full of nails. The saw dug into a big spike and threw him clear across the room. "Of course, I've never used them on nails before, sir." Six months later, just when the instructor was on the verge of taking stress leave, Marty and Gerard graduated.

Marty immediately had an idea for using their newly acquired skills. "Gerard, let's build a house."

Gerard thought about the idea. "Marty, I'll tell you what. Why don't you build a house, and I'll build a house, then we'll decide which one to live in, okay?" Marty agreed, and he immediately began searching for a place to build. He found a beautiful spot down at Booga Beach. The view was spectacular, the sand was soft, and the building material was abundant. He framed and paneled his house with whatever he could find—mostly driftwood—and in one week he had it built.

In the meantime, Gerard had drawn up some plans of his own, and he decided that instead of building on the sand he would build on a rocky outcropping, a stone's throw from Marty's house.

Gerard wanted to lay a solid foundation, and with the rocky landscape as rough as it was, he decided he would have to blast. He pulled out his custom cordless Holtmeister rock-coring drill, and then drilled two holes. He filled the first one with Kapowee rods. Then he lit the fuse. KAPOWSKI!!! Bits of rock and debris shot into the air and showered onto the beach. Marty was sleeping on his deck when the blast sounded, and the boom jolted him high into the air. He came down hard, landing on his head. He walked over to Gerard, covered in dirt and dust.

"Uh, Gerard—"

"Marty, look out!"

A big chunk of rock that had shot up was now coming down. Gerard was wearing a hard hat. Marty wasn't. Unfortunately for Marty, he was the target. SMACK! The rock hit him square on the head.

For the second blast, Marty put a hard hat over the bump on his head, then stood underneath Gerard.

"I'm not taking any chances this time," Marty said.

Gerard ignited the blast and the Kapowee rods exploded.

BABABOOOM!! The blast rocked the countryside and shook the waters of Booga Bay.

"I used a few extra Kapowee rods for that one," Gerard said as bits and pieces of rock came clinking down. When the rock shower finally settled, Marty stepped out from under Gerard. He removed his hard hat and wiped his brow.

"Phew, I'm sure glad that's over," Marty sighed.

Unfortunately for Marty, the blast had sent another rock high into the air, and it was now coming down. Marty looked up. "Uh, oh . . ." CLUNK! The second bump on his head was bigger than the first.

Two lumps in my coffee is more than enough for this little monkey, Marty thought as he stumbled to his feet, then headed for home.

Over the next several weeks, Gerard continued to work hard, and on the final day of summer his house was finished. He had just driven the last nail when Booga Booga Land was hit by a torrential rainstorm. Furious winds howled and lakes of water came pouring down from the sky.

Gerard was inside of his house sleeping soundly, when a loud crack of thunder awoke him. He looked outside. *I'm sure glad I built my house on a rock,* he thought. *Poor Marty. Oh no . . .* Gerard rushed outside and down to the beach. When he got to where Marty's house had been, the water was up to his shoulders and there was no sign of the little monkey. The only things Gerard saw were a few bits and pieces of Marty's house, scattered in the trees and along the shoreline. Gerard began searching for his little friend. All night he searched, until finally, at dawn, he spotted something floating in the distance. As he approached, he saw Marty, still asleep, and lying on his bed. Gerard stuck out a hoof and shook Marty on the shoulder. "Marty! Marty! Wake up!"

Marty woke up.

"Gerard, what are you doing in my house?"

"I'm not in your house, Marty. And I've got news for you: you're not in it either."

Marty looked around. "Good Gimbo! Did I leave the tap on again?" It took awhile for Marty to realize what had happened.

As Gerard towed Marty safely to shore, Marty reflected, "I guess my house was kind of like a sandcastle, huh, Gerard? The tide came in, and the house fell."

"That's right, Marty, but look on the bright side. At least now we don't have to decide whose house to live in. Come on, let's go check out your new castle."

As Marty and Gerard raced up the hill to their new house, Marty smiled as he thought to himself, *I sure am glad I have a friend like Gerard!*

The Parable of the Wise and Foolish Builders
(Matthew 7:24-27)

Therefore everyone who hears these words of mine and puts them into practice is like a wise man who built his house on the rock. The rain came down, the streams rose, and the winds blew and beat against that house; yet it did not fall, because it had its foundation on the rock.

But everyone who hears these words of mine and does not put them into practice is like a foolish man who built his house on sand. The rain came down, the streams rose, and the winds blew and beat against that house, and it fell with a great crash.

In this parable Jesus speaks of two men, one who was wise and the other who wasn't. The wise man built his house on the rock, just like Gerard did, and the foolish man built his house on the sand, just like Marty. Jesus is saying that people who hear His words and put them into practice are like the wise man, and those who hear His words but don't put them into practice are like the foolish man. Jesus did a lot of teaching when He was here on earth, and when He taught he wanted to let people know how they could live the best life possible. His teachings are guidelines that have stood the test of time. So put the teachings of Jesus into practice, and when the storms of life blow, you will have a house that will not fall.

THREE
No Light in the Lighthouse

It was a fine Booga Booga Land morning, the kind of morning that Marty and Gerard just loved to wake up to. They jumped out of bed, and, not even bothering to change out of their pajamas, they ran outside. The sun was just beginning to peek over the horizon, and when the first ray of sunlight bolted toward them, Marty excitedly jumped up in the air and caught it.

"I've got it. That's four days in a row for me!"

"You're not playing fair, Marty. You jumped," Gerard whined.

"Gerard, you're eighteen feet tall. Now, do you want a full orchestra, or will one violin do?"

They went into the house to get their breakfast bowls, and then returned to eat their cereal in the warm sunlight. As they were crunching on their cereal and looking out across Booga Bay, Marty suddenly spotted something.

"Gerard, I think I see a ship!"

"Marty, there are no ships in Booga Bay. There have never been ships in Booga Bay."

"Okay then, what's *that*?" Marty pointed into the bay.

"*That*, Marty, is a Coconut Crispy on your nose."

Marty wiped the Crispy off, then went into the house for more cereal. "Gerard, there's no more cereal!"

"Sorry, Marty, I emptied the box. Could you remember to get me two dozen leaves when you go to the store?"

"Who said anything about going to the store?" Marty said as he came back outside.

"You need Coconut Crispies, don't you?" Marty got his wagon, and then began trudging toward the store.

As he was returning home, he noticed the prize in the box was a Woogee Wadget. Marty loved Woogee Wadgets, and he couldn't resist digging into the box. Coconut Crispies spilt all over the sidewalk as he stuffed his hand in and thrashed around. Not being able to find the prize with his hand, he decided to use his head.

Unfortunately, he got his head stuck in the box, and he staggered around, bouncing off of people, poles, and parking meters. He still had the box on his head when he arrived home and banged into their front door. That gave him an idea. "Gerard, I think we should build a lighthouse."

Gerard thought about the idea. "Marty, I'm not sure Booga Booga Land needs a lighthouse right now. By the way, did you remember my leaves?"

"Leaves?" Marty had a blank look on his face.

"Marty, I asked you to get me two dozen leaves, remember?"

"Two dozen! Gerard, I only have ten fingers, you know. How am I supposed to remember that many?"

Gerard gave an understanding sigh. He was beginning to realize that Marty was a special monkey, and with him around, life would always be full of surprises.

Over the next few days, Marty continued to pester Gerard about the lighthouse idea, until he finally had Gerard convinced they should build one. They made a few plans and then began the task of looking for a suitable building spot.

"What do you think of this place?" Marty asked as he looked down at Gerard from the top of a coconut tree.

"Marty, trees are not for lighthouses. And besides, I don't think our neighbors would appreciate a lighthouse in their backyard."

They eventually found a spot on a rocky reef, overlooking Booga Bay. Gerard looked at the pile of rugged rocks, then looked at his little monkey friend. Marty knew what that meant. Those rocks had to be leveled. It was time to blast. Gerard pulled out his custom cordless Holtmeister rock-coring drill, and Marty quickly began searching for a hard hat. He eventually found one, and, to make sure it wouldn't come off, he glued it to his head.

"Hey, Gerard, look!" Marty shouted. "I don't have to worry about rocks hitting me this time. I glued the hard hat to my head."

Gerard looked down at Marty. Marty looked up at Gerard.

"Whaaat? You don't think it's going to come off, do you?"

"No, Marty, I don't. And when it's time to take it off, give me a call, okay?" Marty had a puzzled look on his face. He knew Gerard was on to something, but he couldn't figure out just what.

Gerard grabbed the T-handle of the detonation box and began the countdown. "Three, two, one . . ." He pushed down, but nothing happened. He tried again. Still nothing. Marty poked his head out from behind some rocks. "Maybe there's something wrong with the Kapowee rods, Gerard. I'll go check." Marty scrambled out from behind the rocks and ran toward the rods. "I think I found the problem, Gerard—loose wires."

"Marty, don't touch those—" Gerard's caution came too late, and the rods exploded. BABOOOOOM!! When the rocks and debris finally settled, Marty was nowhere to be seen. Gerard began to search for his little friend. Then he heard Marty's unmistakable, wavering call coming from the sky. By the time Gerard looked up, Marty was already coming down. Gerard stuck out his front hooves and prepared to catch the little monkey. He had Marty all lined up for the grab, when—THUD!—Marty went right through Gerard's outstretched hooves and sailed headlong into the ground.

"Sorry, Marty. I really thought I had you this time."

"You know, Gerard, it's a good thing I had my hard hat on. That could have hurt."

Over the next several days, construction of the lighthouse continued on at a steady pace; the little monkey and the tall giraffe worked with enthusiasm and energy to complete the job. Marty was in charge of making sure the lighthouse stood straight, but in the end—and in typical Marty style—the lighthouse stood like a bent banana.

Gerard looked at the lighthouse. Then he looked down at Marty.

"Don't look at me, Gerard," Marty said. "I think I had a bad plumb line." Regardless of how the lighthouse looked, at least it was finished, and ships now had a way to navigate the treacherous waters leading into Booga Bay.

On opening night, Marty and Gerard gazed into the darkness as they received word that a ship carrying a fresh load of sardines was heading their way. They spotted the ship's glimmering lights, and as they fixed their eyes on the faint glow, a very strange thing happened. The ship's lights went out. Gerard squinted into the darkness. "I don't see the ship's lights, Marty. You don't think it sunk, do you?"

"Of course not, Gerard. They just turned out their lights to get some sleep."

The next morning as Marty and Gerard were having breakfast, pieces of a ship began floating ashore. A few moments later, there was a knock on the lighthouse door. Marty answered. It was a wet Stan with his wet shaggy dog, Rufus.

"Hi, Stan. What brings you here?" Marty asked.

"Mostly the backstroke, but I did use the sidestroke a few times," Stan said, trying to make light of the situation.

Gerard came down the stairs to see what was going on. "Stan, what a pleasant surprise! Looking for a window-washing job?"

"No, actually, I'm the captain of a sardine ship now—or at least I was, until it sank last night. I thought your lighthouse was operating."

"It is, Stan. Didn't you see the lights?"

"The only thing I saw were our sardines, and they swam away faster than lizards hit by lightning."

Gerard looked down at Marty. "Marty, you *did* install the lights, right?"

"Of course I did, Gerard. I took the bulbs from this box, the one that says—oops . . . 'For flashlight use only.'" The next day Gerard installed the proper bulbs, and the lighthouse was in operation.

It was a week later when the next ship showed up. Marty and Gerard stared into the darkness as the lights of the ship flickered in the distance. Just then Marty had an idea. "Gerard, I'm going to polish our lights, just to make sure that ship sees them." Marty went into the lighthouse beam room and returned a short time later. "That ship should be able to see our lights now, Gerard."

"I suppose," Gerard said, "if there was a ship to see them." Marty looked out across the ocean. The ship's lights had disappeared.

"Marty, I think we just lost another ship. You must have blocked the light."

"That's impossible, Gerard. I had them turned off!"

Gerard looked down at Marty. Marty looked up at Gerard.

Hmm, Marty thought, *I wonder if I did something wrong?*

The next morning there was a knock on their lighthouse door. Marty looked out the window and could see what appeared to be an old man and a shaggy dog. "Gerard, I think it's for you." Gerard went down and answered the door. "Stan! Don't tell me that was your ship that went down again!"

"Yep. And we lost another load of sardines, but at least it's not as bad as last time. I put them in cans this time."

As Stan and Rufus walked away, Gerard said, "Marty, I think Stan is getting pretty good at doing the backstroke by now, and he really doesn't need any more practice. Maybe it's time we let someone else run the lighthouse. What do you think?" Marty thought about Gerard's idea, then agreed, and the next day their lighthouse was sold.

That night, Marty and Gerard reflected on their lighthouse experience over a delicious supper of lishkenpopple stew and coconut cream pie. When they were finished eating, they jumped into their bunks and Marty pulled out his flashlight. He zoomed the beam across the ceiling and around the room.

"Marty, what are you doing?"

"I'm letting my light shine, Gerard. I don't want any more ships to sink."

A few hours later, when Marty's batteries finally ran out, he peeked over the edge of his bunk. "Gerard, do you have any more flashlight batteries?"

"Go to sleep, Marty."

"Oookay, I'll take that as a no."

Gerard settled back into his bunk, and then began snoring. As Marty listened to Gerard's snores, which sounded like hoots coming from a ship's foghorn, he looked over the edge of his bunk and thought, *I guess that ship is anchored for the night.* Marty then plunked his head onto his pillow and began tooting like a little tugboat as he, too, sailed serenely off to sleep.

The Parable of the Lamp under a Bowl

(Matthew 5:14-16)

You are the light of the world. A city on a hill cannot be hidden. Neither do people light a lamp and put it under a bowl. Instead they put it on its stand, and it gives light to everyone in the house. In the same way, let your light shine before men, that they may see your good deeds and praise your Father in heaven.

In this parable Jesus is saying that His followers are to demonstrate the love of God by doing good deeds for others. God knows that it would be a dark world without someone shining the light of His love, so He's asked His followers to light up the world by doing good deeds. Just as the purpose of a lighthouse is to give light so that ships can be guided safely into port, God wants His followers to let their lives shine with His love so that people can be guided to Him.

FOUR
The Booga Bolter

It was a gorgeous day in Booga, and Marty and Gerard were smiling as they walked back from Monty's Malt and Milkshake Shop. Marty was sampling his extra large ice cream cone, and Gerard was gulping down his frosty chocolate shake. They were passing by a seafood restaurant run by Squid Sushi, when Marty noticed a sign in the window: "See Diverse One-Toed Squid."

"Gerard, hit the brakes. I've got to see this squid." Gerard stopped and waited, while Marty ran toward the restaurant.

Unfortunately, Marty tripped on the front step and went sailing headlong into the closed door. His ice cream cone went flying, and when Mr. Sushi opened the door, it hit him on the nose. "Did someone knock? Hmm, vanilla, my favorite."

"It was me, Mr. Sushi," Marty said as he picked himself up off the front step. "I want to see that squid." Mr. Sushi gave Marty a puzzled look. Marty then looked up at the sign.

"Oh," said Mr. Sushi, "it's supposed to say, 'Sea Divers Wanted, Squid.' I guess the printer misunderstood me when I called him. You see, Marty, my shipment of sardines sank the other day, and I need a couple of divers to recover them."

Marty went over to Gerard, talked the matter over, and then returned. "Squid, you're looking at two of Booga Booga Land's finest divers."

"Splendid," Squid said. "You're hired. By the way, the skipper of my boat is an ex-sardine ship captain, and his shaggy dog has agreed to come along as an extra diver. You should also know the goal of my mission. I want to recover all of the sardine cans. One hundred cans went down, and one hundred cans must come up."

The next day, the snorkelers and their skipper headed out to sea. Their boat was equipped with sardine can sonar, and it didn't take long for them to locate the sunken cargo. Marty was the first one overboard. "Kowabunga!" he shouted as he plunged into the water. Rufus was next. "Woof," he barked. Gerard was last.

"Ouch!" he hollered as he hit the bottom. The water was only knee-deep for him.

Gerard was recovering the sardine cans rather easily. He walked around, poked his head in the water, and picked the cans up with his mouth. Rufus and Marty, on the other hand, were swimming around frantically looking for the cans—well, at least Rufus was. Marty was spending most of his time playing around, and he frequently had to be reminded of the goal of the mission.

At the end of the first day, Gerard had recovered forty cans, Rufus had recovered ten, and Marty had none.

On the second day, Marty found a can. It was located at the entrance to the cave of an electric Booga Bolter. This was a job for . . . Rufus.

"Rufus, I found a can of sardines for you. Do you think you can get it?"

Rufus looked at the can. It was a long way down, but he was up for the challenge. Unfortunately, Rufus did not see the cave. Taking a deep breath, he dove down. As Rufus reached to get the can, the Bolter emerged. Rufus received a monstrous electric jolt, sending him flying out of the water and into the boat. Marty recovered the can and brought it to Stan.

"Good work, Marty," Stan said. He then looked over at Rufus. "It's not time for a break yet, Rufus. Back to work." Rufus barked out a trite "Woof" (dog talk for "Stan, I've been hooped!"). Rufus then trudged to the edge of the boat and jumped back into the water.

Over the next few days all of the sardine cans were recovered, except for one. Squid now had ninety-nine cans, but there was still that one missing. Days and days passed as the search continued.

Squid added extra sonar power to the boat, along with a sardine-can imaging scanner. After weeks of searching, the missing can was finally found. It was lodged in a deep rock crevice, inaccessible to the divers.

"We're going to have to blast," Gerard announced as he assessed the situation. Marty frantically began searching for a hard hat, but, unable to find one, he taped his lunch pail to his head.

Gerard looked down at Marty. Marty looked up at Gerard.

"Whaaat? Don't you think it's going to work?"

"It'll work just fine," Gerard said, as he began filling the crevice with plastic Kapowee rods.

When everyone had taken cover, Gerard detonated the blast.

KABOOOOM!! The explosion thundered across the water and echoed across the land. Water sprayed, rocks flew, and the can of sardines went soaring high into the air. Marty spotted the can and reached over the side of the boat to catch it. Unfortunately, he missed, and the can of sardines bounced off of his lunch bucket. Marty went sprawling into the water.

The can of sardines, unfortunately for the crew, was also now back in the water—and tightly wedged under a rock ledge. Gerard assessed the situation again. "It looks like we're going to have to—"

"Wait a minute," Marty interrupted as he looked at the dent in his lunch pail. "Why don't we just use the hydraulic Jack-Em-Up?" Marty was getting tired of being hit on the head every time Gerard blasted. To Marty's relief, the crew accepted his idea.

Gerard positioned the Jack-Em-Up under the rock while Marty jumped on the controls. As Marty started lifting the rock, he looked at the crew. "Okay, now someone has to go down there. Any volunteers?"

No one volunteered.

"Uh, Marty, maybe you should let Stan operate the Jack-Em-Up," Gerard suggested.

"Whaaat? Don't you trust me?"

"It's not that, Marty. Well . . . on second thought, that's exactly it." Marty handed the controls over to Stan. Then he asked, "Now, who's going to go down to get the can?" Everyone looked at him.

"Oookay, I guess that matter is settled. Just be careful with those controls, Stan."

Marty dove down, and just as he was about to grab the can, he felt a nudge on his shoulder. He looked over and saw the Booga Bolter. The Bolter held nothing back as it blasted Marty with a massive, super-charged bolt. Marty flew out of the water holding the can of sardines, then watched as Stan, Rufus, and Gerard faded out of sight. A few minutes later he reentered the atmosphere, heading straight for the boat.

"I've got you!" Gerard called out.

"Move the boat, Stan!" Marty shouted back. Marty would rather take his chances hitting the water than slipping through Gerard's hooves again. As Marty flew past the boat, he threw the can of sardines to Gerard. Gerard caught the can and watched as the little monkey cannonballed into the water. SPLOOSH! BLUB! BLUB! Minutes later, Marty resurfaced and climbed back into the boat.

That night, with the mission accomplished, Squid held a huge celebration party at his restaurant. He was so happy he could hardly contain himself. "Sardine sushi and banana salad for everyone!" he shouted. The celebration went well into the night, and it was early morning before Marty and Gerard finally arrived home.

"I wonder why Squid wouldn't settle for ninety-nine cans?" Marty said as he jumped into his bunk.

"I guess he just loves sardines, Marty. And when you love sardines, every can is a treasure."

The Parable of the Lost Sheep

(Luke 15:4-7)

Suppose one of you has a hundred sheep and loses one of them. Does he not leave the ninety-nine in the open country and go after the lost sheep until he finds it?

And when he finds it, he joyfully puts it on his shoulders and goes home. Then he calls his friends and neighbors together and says, "Rejoice with me; I have found my lost sheep." I tell you that in the same way there will be more rejoicing in heaven over one sinner who repents than over ninety-nine righteous persons who do not need to repent.

In this parable, Jesus is saying that all people need to repent of their sins, whether they think they need to or not. Some people may think that, because they live such good lives, they don't need to repent, but they are in the same boat as any other sinner. Everyone needs to repent. God rejoices when people repent, not only because they've come into a right relationship with Him, but also because they will one day be with Him in heaven. The message of this parable can be summed up in another way. Sin is like trash, and it needs to be thrown out. The good news is, God has a big trashcan, and it's big enough to take everyone's sins—no matter how big or how many. So if you have a pile of sins that are cluttering up your life, throw them into God's trashcan. You'll rejoice, and heaven will too!

FIVE
Squid Sushi Loses His Marbles

It was the dawning of another beautiful day in Booga, and the sun was sparkling like a diamond as its brilliant rays spread across the land. It was a special day for Marty, and he quickly gulped down his breakfast, rushed to his room, and put on his diving mask and flippers. He then went to the front door and waited for Gerard. When Gerard finally came, Marty excitedly shuffled out the door, jumping up and down like a penguin on hot coals. He and Gerard were going swimming.

They made their way down to the pier at Booga Bay, and when they arrived, Marty looked down the long pier. Then he prepared for takeoff. He raced down the runway with his flippers sounding like the propellers of an airplane. When he reached the end of the pier, he jumped wildly into the air. Unfortunately for Marty, the tide was out, and he made a crash landing on the rocky reef far below.

"Oookay, that kind of hurt," he said as he stumbled to his feet, and then looked up at Gerard. "Gerard, I have an idea."

"I know, you want to buy a parachute, right?"

"No . . . I was thinking we should ask Mr. Sushi if he wants to add oysters to his menu."

Gerard wondered where that idea came from, then asked, "Do you see any down there?"

"I'm not sure. What do they look like?"

"They have a whitish-gray wavy layered shell, and they're about the size of a sardine can."

"Oh, forget it then. This thing is slimy and has eight legs."

Marty threw the octopus back onto the reef.

Marty continued to pester Gerard about the oyster idea, until finally Gerard agreed. The next day they went to Squid Sushi's seafood restaurant to see if Squid was interested. Squid liked their proposal, thinking oyster omelets would be a tasty addition to his succulent sardine sandwiches.

Marty and Gerard immediately began their search for an oyster bed, and, to their surprise, they found one right in Booga Bay. They wasted no time in setting up their operation. Gerard collected and tossed the oysters, while Marty caught them in his baseball mitt and stockpiled them on the beach. When they had enough for their first load, they rented a dump truck, and then tossed the oysters in. Marty quickly jumped into the driver's seat. Gerard looked down at Marty.

Marty looked up at Gerard. "Whaaat? I've driven before."

"Marty, driving a tricycle and driving a truck are two different things."

"Okay, if you can get in the cab, then you can drive." Gerard looked inside the small cab, then realized Marty was right. It was too small. Gerard hopped into the back of the truck and hung on tightly.

The truck got off to a wobbly start as Marty popped the clutch and jerked the truck forward. Oysters spilled onto the beach, and Gerard almost did too. When Marty shifted from first to second, the truck jerked again, spilling more oysters. The truck lurched a lot, but Gerard didn't say a thing. The truck, however, seemed to stutter out the words, "Clutch out slow, then I'll go."

Marty almost rolled the truck at the first corner. He spilled more oysters, and this time Gerard was thrown off of the truck. As Marty neared Squid's restaurant, there were hardly any oysters left. He was stopped at a red light when Gerard came running up from behind and jumped back into the box. As Marty started to go, he hit the dump lever instead of first gear, and the few oysters remaining in the truck, along with Gerard, dumped onto the road.

When Marty finally arrived at Squid's, he got out to check on the oysters. He was surprised to see Gerard come running up to the truck, out of breath.

"Marty, you dumped all of the oysters onto the streets. We've got to go back."

Marty checked the box. Gerard was right. It was empty.

As they retraced their path, they discovered something very strange. All the oysters were gone, but the streets were full of Booga people playing marbles. Marty took a closer look at one of the marbles, trying to figure out what had happened.

Meanwhile, Gerard had a hunch regarding the mystery. He went back to Booga Bay and cracked open an oyster. There, nestled inside the shell, he found a marble just like the ones the people had been playing with. He looked down at Marty. "Marty, I think I know what happened to all of those oysters."

As they were sitting there wondering what to do, Marty came up with an idea. "Gerard, I think Booga Booga Land needs a marble shop." It didn't take long for Gerard to be convinced that Marty was right, and the very next day, Marty and Gerard's Big Booga Marble Company opened for business.

Their business took off like a rocket, as marble mania began to spread across Booga Booga Land. Soon everyone was playing, collecting, or trading the little gems. Squid Sushi even started a collection and was quickly swallowed up by the craze. He was fascinated by the exquisite marbles, and it wasn't long before he had the finest collection in all of the land.

One day as Marty and Gerard were opening oysters, they discovered a rare marble. It radiated with the colors of the rainbow, and it was ten times the size of any other. Word of their discovery soon got out, and collectors from everywhere began flocking to Booga to get a glimpse of their magnificent find. Squid Sushi even came. He took one look at the jewel and was overcome by its splendor. He had to have it. "How much?" he asked.

Marty and Gerard hadn't thought of selling it, but they huddled together to discuss the matter. After a short while Marty emerged from the huddle. "It's not for sale, Squid."

Squid had to have that marble. "I'll give you my entire collection of marbles," he said.

Marty went back into the huddle and soon emerged again.

"We're still not selling it, Squid."

Squid was bent on getting that marble. He thought for a moment, and then said, "You can have everything I have—my collection and my restaurant business."

Marty went back into the huddle. "You know, Gerard, Squid's offer sounds like a fair deal to me. Everything he has, for this measly marble. What do you think?" Marty and Gerard went over to Squid. "It's a deal."

Squid was ecstatic. He danced around and jumped in the air.

"Squid, have you lost all of your marbles?" people asked as they saw him cha-cha and twist in the streets.

Marty and Gerard were pretty happy themselves. They held a celebration dinner that evening and invited Squid to join them for pineapple pie and coconut milkshakes. They celebrated well into the night, and by the time they went home, they were so tired they could hardly keep their pearly peepers open.

"Squid sure was happy," Marty said as he started drifting off to sleep. "I wonder what made him dance around so much? After all, it was only a measly marble."

"Marty, I think it was much more than just a measly marble to him. I think it was the treasure he'd been looking for, and to him, it was priceless.

The Parable of the Valuable Pearl

(Matthew 13:45-46)

Again, the kingdom of heaven is like a merchant looking for fine pearls. When he found one of great value, he went away and sold everything he had and bought it.

In this parable Jesus speaks of a man who was always on the lookout for fine pearls. One day he found a pearl so valuable that he sold everything he had just to buy it. This pearl represents entrance into the kingdom of heaven, and, although you can't buy your way into heaven, you must be willing to give up everything you have. It really shouldn't be such a big deal, though, because if you could compare what you have here on earth with what awaits you in heaven, you'd realize that what you're really doing is giving up nothing and gaining everything.

SIX
The Flaming Monkey

The sun was shining brightly over Booga as Marty and Gerard stepped into their backyard. Gerard went over to relax in his lawn chair, while Marty found the barbecue. As Marty pulled out the matches, they began discussing how to run their newly acquired business, Squid's Seafood Restaurant.

"I wanna be the chef," Marty piped up as he lit the barbeque then put a coconut on the grill.

"Marty, maybe it would be better if you let me handle the cooking duties, okay?"

"Whaaat? Don't you think I can cook?"

"It's not that, Marty." The coconut exploded. "Well, on second thought, that's exactly it." It was soon decided Gerard would be the chef, and Marty would handle the duties of headwaiter.

As they were talking, they also decided to make a few other changes. The first of these changes was to the restaurant's roof. It had to be raised to accommodate an eighteen-foot-tall giraffe.

The next change was to the menu. It was changed from sardines and oysters to specialty burgers and tossed salads. Gerard had an idea for a special one-of-a-kind burger, and Marty was working on an idea to toss salad using firecrackers. The final change was to the restaurant's name. Gerard decided to call it "The Flaming Monkey."

"How come we're calling it 'The Flaming Monkey' and not 'The Flaming Monkey *and* Giraffe'?" Marty asked.

"You'll just have to wait and see," Gerard said.

On opening day, there was a huge crowd. Marty stood at the door in his new tuxedo and watched as the people filed in. When they were all seated, Marty began to take their orders. He walked into the kitchen with the first order of the day. It was for one of Gerard's specialty burgers.

"One special coming right up!" Gerard said as he poured his gourmet gravy on the patty then gave it to Marty.

"What's this?" Marty asked.

"It's a flaming monkey!" Gerard said as he put a match to the burger and it exploded into flames.

Marty dashed out of the kitchen with the flames shooting left, right, up, and down. When he arrived at the table, the burger was still blazing. He quickly emptied a bottle of catsup on the blaze, then waited for the smoke to clear. To the delight of the patron—and to Marty's relief—the burger was perfectly cooked, and it was tastily flavored too.

In the following weeks, Marty and Gerard experimented with different extinguishing sauces and running speeds. Soon they could accommodate the preferences of any patron. News of their restaurant spread throughout the land, and it wasn't long before the Flaming Monkey became known as the best eating place in all of Booga Booga Land.

One day their restaurant received an unexpected call. It was from the president of Booga Booga Land, Bob Booga. Marty answered the phone in his usual manner. "Hello, this is the Flaming Monkey, Marty speaking."

The voice on the other end said, "Hello, Marty. This is Bob Booga, the president of Booga Booga Land." Marty sat up in his chair. He couldn't believe the president was calling. Bob continued. "I was wondering if I could book a banquet at your business?"

"Just hold on, Bob." Marty called Gerard over and whispered, "It's the president!"

Gerard calmly took the phone. "Hello, this is Gerard speaking."

"Hello, Gerard. This is Bob Booga. I would like to book a banquet for my daughter's wedding, and I was wondering if your restaurant would be suitable for serving, say, six hundred dignitaries?"

"I think we can handle six hundred, sir," Gerard said as he looked down at Marty. Marty looked up at Gerard and nodded. "No problem, Gerard. I think I have a fire extinguisher and a flame-retardant suit somewhere around here."

Over the next several months, Marty and Gerard made preparations for the big banquet. They ordered a truckload of cows and enough burger sauce to put out a flaming high-rise.

When the big day came, they were ready. The restaurant was decorated with banners and the tables were set with fine cutlery. Marty was dressed in a flame-retardant tuxedo and stood at the door.

The first ones to arrive were Bob and his daughter Betty. His stretch limousine pulled up in front of the restaurant and was followed by another carrying the groom, Benny Bittleman. They now waited for the arrival of the dignitaries. They waited and waited.

And waited some more. No one came. Bob phoned his office. "Where is everyone?" he asked. To his surprise, he discovered that all the guests had turned down their invitations.

Benny and Betty sat down in the empty restaurant. They were deeply disappointed. Marty tried to console them, as Bob told his workers to personally go out and invite the guests again. Bob explained the situation to Marty and Gerard and said there would be a delay of a day or two, while the matter was being resolved.

"No problem," Gerard said. "We'll just let the cows walk around a little longer."

Two days later, Bob received more bad news. The invited dignitaries didn't care about the wedding. Most of them were on business trips or on vacation. Others slammed their doors in the faces of Bob's workers—or told them to take an eight-day walk off of a seven-day week. The cows also pressured Bob; they were getting tired of walking around and threatened to go to another banquet.

"What am I going to do?" Bob asked, bewildered.

"I've got an idea," Marty said. "I could invite some friends from my old hometown, that is, if you don't mind monkeys."

"And I could invite some people from Toosmallforme," Gerard said.

"Splendid," Bob said. "And I'll put the word out on the street."

Soon Bob had his people on the streets inviting everyone they could find. Beggars, bankers, marble players, the rich, and the poor. Everyone was invited.

As the guests came through the door, each one was given a bottle of their favorite burger sauce. No one was allowed in unless they had a bottle of sauce. When everyone was seated, the banquet began. Flames flew, music played, sauce flowed, and people laughed. The banquet was going delightfully well, until Marty brought a flaming burger to a guest who had no sauce. Marty quickly put out the flame. Then he called Bob over.

"How did you get into the banquet without a bottle of sauce?" Bob asked. The guest didn't reply. Bob looked the man square in the eyes. "No one is allowed in here without a bottle of sauce. You know that, don't you?" The guest still didn't reply. Bob could see he had a troublemaker on his hands. He looked over at Marty. "Marty, could you please escort this impostor to the door?"

As Marty was escorting the flimflam man to the door, Gerard poked his head out of the kitchen. He looked down at Marty, then over at the impostor. "Marty, it looks like you could use one of these," Gerard said as he threw a Kapowee rod to the doorway.

As everyone took cover, Marty threw the rod outside and closed the door on the impostor. "This is your free trip out of Booga Booga Land," Marty said as the rod exploded. BABABOOOM! The scalawag was sent flying across the ocean and onto the gloomy island of Losta Sola.

"Splendid," Bob said as the banquet continued in a festive fashion, free of further flare-ups—save for the occasional burger.

The banquet ended late in the evening, and Marty and Gerard were exhausted by the time they got home. As Marty was hopping into his bunk, he commented, "Gerard, all those guys who turned down their invitations sure missed out, didn't they?"

"They sure did, Marty."

"And so did that scalawag of an impostor, huh, Gerard?"

"Him too."

Marty pulled his covers up over his head and tucked himself in as Gerard turned out the lights. They said their "good nights," and a moment later the room was filled with the woos and wees of soft snores, as the little waiter and the big chef serenely drifted off to sleep.

The Parable of the Wedding Banquet
(Matthew 22:2-14)

The kingdom of heaven is like a king who prepared a wedding banquet for his son. He sent his servants to those who had been invited to the banquet to tell them to come, but they refused to come.

Then he sent some more servants and said, "Tell those who have been invited that I have prepared my dinner: My oxen and fattened cattle have been butchered, and everything is ready. Come to the wedding banquet."

But they paid no attention and went off—one to his field, another to his business. The rest seized his servants, mistreated them and killed them. The king was enraged.

He sent his army and destroyed those murderers and burned their city.

Then he said to his servants, "The wedding banquet is ready, but those I invited did not deserve to come. Go to the street corners and invite to the banquet anyone you find." So the servants went out into the streets and gathered all the people they could find, both good and bad, and the wedding hall was filled with guests.

But when the king came in to see the guests, he noticed a man there who was not wearing wedding clothes. "Friend," he asked, "how did you get in here without wedding clothes?" The man was speechless.

Then the king told the attendants, "Tie him hand and foot, and

> throw him outside, into the darkness, where there will be weeping and gnashing of teeth."
>
> For many are invited, but few are chosen.

In this parable Jesus is talking about heaven. He is saying that although everyone is invited, only those who meet a certain requirement can gain entrance. Just like there was a requirement to be at Bob's banquet, there is a requirement to get to heaven. That requirement is repentance. This same rule applies to everyone. It seems that some people are making their own rules, though, thinking that all you have to do to get to heaven is be a good person. Well, that would be nice, but it's not God's way. So don't make your own rules. Instead, follow God's way, repent, and get in on the Big Banquet.

SEVEN
Wally the Waiter

It was early in the morning and the sun's rays were just beginning to stream over the hills and valleys of Booga Booga Land, as Marty opened his eyes to welcome another day. He stared at the ceiling for a moment, wondering whether to get out of bed or wait for his alarm clock to ring. It was Coconut Crispy day, and Marty had set his alarm clock to beat Gerard to the breakfast table. Unfortunately for Marty, Gerard was already up and in the kitchen, eating breakfast.

"Marty, if you're waiting for your alarm clock to ring, it rang half an hour ago, and I turned it off. By the way, I finished off the Coconut Crispies again."

Marty thumped his head onto his pillow. *It's just not my day*, he thought as he rolled out of bed. He then remembered that he slept on the top bunk, eighteen feet above the floor. He whirled through the air and landed headfirst. Marty stumbled to his feet rubbing his head, then wobbled into the kitchen. "Gerard, I was thinking about something."

"I know. You're going to buy that parachute I was talking about, right?"

"No . . . I was thinking we should become private investigators."

Gerard thought for a moment. "Uh, Marty, who's going to hire us as private investigators?"

"We can ask the president. It seems those government machines always have a loose nut or two somewhere."

After a bit more thought, Gerard agreed with Marty's idea.

The next day, they sold their restaurant, and went to visit Bob, the president of Booga Booga Land.

"I have just the job for you," Bob explained. "We've had a breach of security in our staff cafeteria. Top-secret chocolate cake and cinnamon bun recipes have gone missing, and I need someone to find the fiend who filched our formulas." Marty and Gerard considered the offer, and then decided to take on the assignment.

The next day, they showed up at the staff cafeteria, disguised in sunglasses. They probed around, questioning one employee then another, carefully bringing up the subject of chocolate cake and cinnamon buns, so as to not arouse suspicion. All of the employees came out as clean as a scrubbed potato except for one, Wally the waiter. He seemed to be a bit agitated by all of the questioning. Marty decided to try and shake Wally up a little bit more. He ordered a piece of chocolate cake from Wally, then another, and another. Each time Marty mentioned the words "chocolate cake," Wally would shudder. Marty continued to order chocolate cake until Wally was shaking so badly he could hardly walk.

That night, Marty and Gerard followed Wally home. They were surprised to discover that his house was actually a huge-walled mansion, a luxury that ordinarily would be far beyond his meager means. The eclectic detectives were on to something, and they decided their next step would be to conduct an investigation of Wally's premises.

The next day, after Wally left for work, Marty and Gerard put on their sunglasses, then strolled up to his mansion. Marty jumped onto Gerard's head and was lifted onto the wall. Just then a police cruiser came around the corner and stopped.

"I had a report of a suspicious-looking monkey and giraffe around here. You two haven't seen anything, have you?" the officer asked.

"Nothing looks suspicious from up here, Officer," Marty said as he adjusted his sunglasses.

"Just thought I'd let you know," the officer said. "Be careful up there now, and let me know if you see anything, okay? You two boys have a fine day now."

After the officer left, Gerard commented, "I think we should talk to Bob about his police force. I'm beginning to think he's got a problem."

Marty looked down from his perch on the wall. "I think you're right, Gerard. Now . . . how do I get down from here?"

"I guess you're going to have to jump," Gerard said. Marty jumped—and landed right beside Gerard. Gerard looked down at Marty. Marty looked up at Gerard. "Whaaat?"

"Marty, we already know what's on *this* side of the wall. You're supposed to jump to the *other* side."

Gerard put Marty back up on the wall, and this time Marty jumped into Wally's yard. He scurried over to the house and into an open window. As he passed through the kitchen, he noticed some cinnamon buns on the counter, along with some chocolate cake crumbs. He continued scampering around until he found Wally's computer. He opened a file called "Chocolate Cake," and there before him was Wally's secret. Wally was selling the recipes and raking in big bamolies from his devious dealings. Marty quickly printed out the information, and then scooted out of the house, stopping only once as he was tempted by the cinnamon buns. When he got to the wall, he discovered he had no way to get back. "Hey, Gerard. Gerard? Are you there?"

"What is it, Marty?"

"How do I get back?"

Gerard thought for a moment, and then came up with an idea. "Is there a garbage can nearby?"

"No. There's only a lawn tractor and a rubber duck."

"No problem," Gerard said. "Jump onto the tractor and use these." Gerard threw two Kapowee rods over the wall, and Marty put them under the tractor.

"By the way, Marty, did you find anything?"

"I think we've got our man," Marty said as he hopped onto the tractor, then lit the Kapowee rods. KAPOWSKI! The tractor rocketed into the sky.

The explosion attracted the police officer, and he pulled his cruiser up to Gerard. "Did you hear anything around here?" the officer asked.

"Yes, sir, and it sounded like it came from inside the wall. Maybe it's that monkey and giraffe you're after."

The explosion had blown a hole in the wall, and the officer went over to investigate. Just then Gerard looked up and saw Marty coming down. "Sir, I think you should get in there right away." The officer squeezed through the hole and into Wally's yard, just as the tractor came down. CRASH! It landed on the roof of his cruiser.

"What was that?" the officer asked.

"Just a lawn tractor, sir." Marty and Gerard quickly fixed the cruiser's roof. Then they hurried off to find Bob.

Bob looked at their findings. "Splendid work. I thought Wally might be our man."

Just then the police officer came in. "Mr. President, sir. There's something funny going on at Wally's. I think a rubber duck just blew up his lawn tractor."

"Uh, Bob . . ." Gerard said. "About your police force . . ."

"Yes, I was just getting to that. I was going to ask you two if you wanted to join. We could use a couple of good officers on our team."

"We kind of noticed that, Bob. Thanks for the offer, but we'll pass on that one. Now, about Wally. You'd better get someone out there to round him up, before he gets away." Bob looked at his police officer, and then looked through a list of his other officers. It seemed his police force had never dealt with a matter as tough as this one before. Bob finally looked up at Marty and Gerard. "Uh, you two wouldn't mind doing this one last job, would you?"

Marty and Gerard agreed, and a short time later they brought Wally in. He was arrested, and as punishment for his crime, he was exiled to the desolate island of Losta Sola.

That night as Marty and Gerard retired to their bunks, Marty commented, "Gerard, Wally was kind of like a weed in Bob's garden, wasn't he?"

"He sure was, Marty."

"That's why he got the heave and the ho to Losta Sola, right?"

"That's why he got the ol' heave ho, Marty."

Marty rolled over and pulled the covers up over his head as Gerard turned out the lights. It had been a long day, and with Wally now brought to justice, the two drowsy detectives could finally get a good night's sleep. They closed their eyes, and soon the room was filled with a melody of snores, as the little monkey and the big giraffe quietly drifted off to Snooza Snooza Land.

The Parable of the Weeds

(Matthew 13:24-30)

The kingdom of heaven is like a man who sowed good seed in his field. But while everyone was sleeping, his enemy came and sowed weeds among the wheat, and went away. When the wheat sprouted and formed heads, then the weeds also appeared.

The owner's servants came to him and said, "Sir, didn't you sow good seed in your field? Where then did the weeds come from?"

"An enemy did this," he replied.

The servants asked him, "Do you want us to go and pull them up?"

"No," he answered, "because while you are pulling the weeds, you may root up the wheat with them. Let both grow together until the harvest. At that time I will tell the harvesters: First collect the weeds and tie them in bundles to be burned; then gather the wheat and bring it into my barn."

In this parable, Jesus is saying that life is a struggle between good and evil. It's Satan and his followers, the weeds, up against God and His followers, the wheat. As the parable says, Satan and his followers are the losers in the end, for not only will they be weeded out of this world, but they will also be severely punished. On the other hand, those who follow God will be taken to heaven, where they will be richly rewarded. So don't be duped by the devil. Don't be a weed like Wally. Instead, live for God, and grow up to be a strong stalk of wheat.

EIGHT

Scatter the Seeds Hither and Thither, Some Will Grow and Some Will Wither

It was a scorcher of a day in Booga Booga Land, and the sun was beating down unrelentingly from the clear, blue, summer sky. Marty was sitting in the shade of a coconut tree in his backyard, chiseling away on a piece of wood. Just then Gerard came out of the house and poked his head around the corner. "Marty, I can't find my Yubba tree. You wouldn't happen to know where it is, would you?"

"Was that the little tree sitting on the window sill in the kitchen?"

"That would be the one. Have you seen it?"

"You know, Gerard, that Yubba tree sure would make a great slingshot." Gerard looked at Marty, then looked at the stick in Marty's hand.

"Marty, my Yubba tree!" Gerard took a deep breath, then turned around and walked back into the house.

Hmm, I wonder what's wrong with him, Marty thought as he continued carving away on the Y-shaped stick. When he was finished, he pulled out a pair of suspenders and attached them to his slingshot. *I sure hope Gerard doesn't mind if I use his suspenders,* Marty thought as he put a marble into the slingshot's pocket and fired a shot at their coconut tree. "Bull's-eye!" As Marty reloaded for another shot, he heard a whooshing sound coming from above. His shot had loosened a coconut, and it was now coming down. Marty looked up. "Bull's-eye!" The coconut hit Marty square between the eyes.

Marty staggered into the house. "Gerard, I have an idea."

"I know. Now you want to cut down the coconut tree, right?"

"No . . . I was thinking we should become farmers."

Gerard thought about the idea. The more he thought about it, the more he liked it. It would keep Marty out of trouble, and they just might enjoy the relaxation of country living. So, the very next day, they quit their detective jobs and began looking for a farm.

They spotted a beautiful place just outside of Booga and went to inquire. They were surprised to discover the owners were a couple of old acquaintances: Stan and his shaggy dog, Rufus.

"We couldn't make a go of it," Stan said. "Sardines just don't grow in this soil."

Sardines? Marty thought. *Good Gimbo! I wonder whose idea that was?* He looked over at Rufus.

While Stan and Gerard discussed the sale of the farm, Marty and Rufus went over to the barn. There was an old bale conveyor standing outside, and Marty wondered how fast it would go. He tugged on the starter, then called out to Rufus, "Wanna go for a ride?" Rufus wagged his tail and hopped on. Marty opened the engine to full throttle, and Rufus took off like a wild waheeli snapped by a wet beach towel. The shaggy dog sailed clear through the barn and landed in the neighbor's cow pasture.

A short while later, Gerard announced a deal had been struck for the sale of the farm, and within a few days Marty and Gerard moved in.

Marty had one thing on his mind when he arrived on the farm: driving the tractor. He immediately headed for the barn, found the tractor, and began figuring out how to start it.

Meanwhile, Gerard went into the house and began figuring out what they would need to begin farming.

"We'll need some seed, we'll need a seeder . . ." Gerard looked out the window, ". . . and we might need a new tractor." Gerard rushed out to the barn and arrived just as Marty was trying to find reverse. "Uh, Marty . . ."

"It's okay, Gerard, I know how to drive a tractor."

"Marty, if you drive a tractor like you drive a truck, we're going to have a hole in the barn wall. Now, why don't you go into town and get some seeds, while I check with the neighbor for a seeder?"

Marty turned the tractor off and jumped down from the seat. After Gerard had left, Marty put on his coveralls, grabbed an empty seed bag, and then began trudging toward Booga.

Monkeys were not made to haul seeds, Marty thought. *Tractors were. Besides, what could be so hard about driving a tractor?* He turned around and went back to the barn. After getting the tractor started, he began pulling on the gearshift to find reverse. "I think this is it," he said as he popped the clutch. "Oops, maybe not." The tractor jerked forward, and went right through the barn wall. *I sure hope Gerard doesn't notice that hole*, Marty thought as he drove the tractor out of the farmyard and toward Booga.

When Marty finally arrived at the seed shop, he realized he couldn't stop. He plowed through the front door, drove down the aisle, and took out the back wall as he left. Fortunately, he had snagged a bag of seeds, and it was now dragging behind. He took a shortcut back to the farm and arrived just as Gerard was unharnessing the seeder. Gerard looked at the hole in the barn wall. "Couldn't find reverse, Marty, or just thought the barn didn't have enough doors?"

"Gerard, it wasn't my fault," Marty insisted. "I think there's something wrong with this tractor." Marty went over to check the seed bag and discovered there was nothing in it—except for a big hole. All of the seeds were gone. "Uh, Gerard, there's something wrong with this seed bag too. Could you check it after you've checked the tractor?" Gerard looked down at Marty, then took a deep breath. "It's okay, Marty, we'll look for the seeds in the morning."

During the night, a light rain fell over Booga Booga Land.

When Marty and Gerard awoke the next day, they were in for a pleasant surprise. In their field, along Marty's shortcut, the seeds had already begun to sprout. Healthy green shoots were popping up everywhere. As they retraced Marty's path across their neighbor's cow pasture, more shoots were growing, and as they walked through the Booga gravel pit—they saw even more. There were a lot of seeds sprouting in the gravel pit, and a lot of tractor-tire marks. Gerard looked down at Marty.

"I was just testing the traction, Gerard."

As they continued following Marty's path, they discovered that the only place the seeds weren't growing was on the road. There the Noodle-Nosed Nifnorkels had eaten them. Marty and Gerard decided to leave the seeds where they were, then glean whatever they could at harvest time.

When the crop had finally ripened, they borrowed their neighbor's combine and prepared to harvest the grain. "Can I drive the combine?" Marty asked. Gerard hesitated, then said, "Uh, Marty, maybe it would be better if I just pulled the combine. I'll let you steer, though, okay?" Marty excitedly hopped into the cab and grabbed the steering wheel as Gerard harnessed up the combine.

Pulling the combine was tougher than Gerard had expected, and Marty wasn't helping as he was steering the combine in a path that looked more like a snake than a straight line.

Their field was the first to be harvested, and it wasn't long before the combine was filled to overflowing. The soil was rich, and it produced stalks that were loaded with grain. As Gerard grunted his way further on and into the cow pasture, there was very little grain to glean. The weeds had choked out almost every stalk. When Gerard got to the gravel pit, he stopped. The seedlings, which had started out so well, were now withered. There was nothing left to harvest. Marty poked his head out of the combine.

"What are you waiting for, Gerard? Let's mow the pit."

"Marty, the hill's too steep. And besides, there's nothing to mow."

"I can get the combine down there," Marty insisted. "There's got to be at least a few kernels." Against Gerard's better judgment, he let Marty take the combine into the gravel pit. Marty raced around the pit. When he was finished, he sped up the side and aired the machine out, landing with a THUD right beside Gerard.

"Let's check the hopper, Gerard!" They both peered into the hopper to see how much grain had been gleaned from the pit.

There was nothing. Not a sniff. Not a kerbobble of a kernel.

"Oookay, I guess I was wrong," Marty admitted.

They arrived home late in the evening, tired and hungry. Gerard pulled out a big dish of peppered pastado and began wolfing it down, while Marty went to the fridge and hauled out a double-decker coconut cream pie. After they were finished eating, Gerard put his elbows on the table and wearily commented, "You know, Marty, that combining sure was a lot of work. Next time I think I'll just let you drive." It had been one long day, and the two tuckered farmers were now ready to hit the hay. They planted themselves in their bunks, then it was "Good night, sleep tight, see you when it's light," as the little monkey and the big giraffe serenely drifted off to Snooza Snooza Land.

The Parable of the Sower and the Soils
(Luke 8:5-8)

A farmer went out to sow his seed. As he was scattering the seed, some fell along the path; it was trampled on, and the birds of the air ate it up. Some fell on rock, and when it came up, the plants withered because they had no moisture. Other seed fell among thorns, which grew up with it and choked the plants. Still other seed fell on good soil. It came up and yielded a crop, a hundred times more than was sown.

In this parable, Jesus is talking about how people respond when they hear the Word of God. Just like there were four soils on which the seeds fell, there are four basic responses that people have.

Response #1: They refuse to believe what they hear. That's the response of hard-hearted people. The Word of God goes out, but it doesn't get a chance to sink into their hearts. It's like the seed the Noodle-Nosed Nifnorkels ate off the road.

Response #2: They believe what they hear, but they only believe it for a little while. These are people who accept what they hear about God, until a little trial comes their way, like someone making fun of their faith. Then they say, "This believing stuff is too hard," and they give it up. These are the stalks choked by weeds.

Response #3: They believe it, but the things of God are not a priority. These people will go to church, unless there's a good football game on TV. They'll tithe, but only if there's money left after buying things for themselves. And they'll do their devotions, that is, if everything else on their daily "to do" list is done first. These are the seedlings on the gravel pit.

Response #4: They totally believe God's Word and apply it to their daily living. This is the response God is looking for, and it comes from a heart that is both good and upright. These are the people who put God first in everything, and who eagerly proclaim His message to others. These are the seeds in the good soil.

NINE
Dough!

It was springtime in Booga Booga Land, and the morning air was filled with the sweet scent of budding trees and blooming flowers. Marty and Gerard were still living on the farm, and Marty was presently in the hayloft, stacking bales beside the loft door. He wiped his brow, then began pushing the bales out the door, sending them tumbling through the air and smashing onto the ground far below. Just then Gerard came out of the house and walked over to the barn. "Marty, what are you doing?"

"I thought I'd surprise you, Gerard. I'm making you mashed hay for breakfast."

Gerard took a mouthful and munched on it. "Hmm . . . it's not bad, Marty, but it could use just a little more mashing."

"More mashing coming right up!" Marty said as he flew out of the loft, taking aim at the pile below. He tumbled through the air and landed, but not exactly as he had planned. For one thing he missed the pile, and for another, he landed on his head. "Oookay, I felt that one," Marty said as he picked himself up and brushed himself off. He looked up at Gerard. "Gerard, I have an idea."

"I know . . . you're thinking of buying a helmet."

"No . . . I was thinking we should sell the farm and open up a bakery."

Gerard thought about the idea. Maybe Marty was right. After all, they had been on the farm for a while now, and a change might do them good. "Okay, Marty, let's sell the farm!"

The very next day they put up a For Sale sign, and the day after that, it was sold.

The characters who bought the farm were "old salties" when it came to farming, and although their past attempts had been unprosperous, they were willing to give it another try. Stan and his shaggy dog, Rufus, were the new owners. "We're not going to plant sardines this time," Stan said. "This time we're planting salmon."

"Oookay," Marty said as he and Gerard left the farm and headed back to Booga. "Someone's really lost their doggy biscuits this time."

It didn't take long for Marty and Gerard to get down to business in Booga, and they soon found a building suitable for their bakery. The building needed a few renovations, and, after installing an eighteen-foot-high ceiling, an oven, two huge flour bins, and a drive-through window, they were ready to start baking. Well, almost ready. There was still the matter of installing a sign.

Gerard assessed the situation, and then looked at Marty. "Marty, I think we're going to have to blast!" Gerard pulled out his custom cordless Holtmeister rock-coring drill, while Marty quickly began searching for a hard hat. Not being able to find one, Marty put a mixing bowl on his head. Marty looked up at Gerard. Gerard looked down at Marty. "I guess it'll do, Marty."

Gerard drilled a huge hole. Then he asked Marty to take the long fuse and string it out behind the building. As Gerard filled the hole with Kapowee rods, he shouted to Marty, "And don't light the fuse until I say it's okay."

From behind the building, the only words Marty heard were ". . . light the fuse . . . it's okay." So he lit the fuse. The fuse sizzled around the building, and by the time Gerard saw the smoking string between his feet it was too late. KABOOOOM!!! Gerard was launched. Marty came around the corner and looked up, only to see Gerard fade into a speck and disappear. Marty looked at the crater in front of the bakery. *Ooo boy! I really did it this time*, he thought. He called the Booga airport to see if Gerard had shown up on their radar screen, but unfortunately, no flying giraffes were reported.

Marty pulled out his telescope. After searching the sky for a few minutes, he spotted the lanky giraffe tumbling through the air. Gerard was on his way down and was coming fast. Unlike Marty, Gerard had no experience in making these kinds of landings.

"Hang on, Gerard!" Marty shouted.

"I would if I had something to hang on to!" Gerard shouted back. Just then Gerard spotted a jumbo jet. He reached out just as the jet was passing by and grabbed onto its wing. The airplane tottered, and the pilot announced, "We're experiencing a bit of turbulence. Everyone please fasten your seat belts." The pilot then looked out of his window and saw Gerard. "Sorry, folks, it's only a giraffe on our wing."

The pilot began to loop and twist the plane, trying to shake Gerard, as the passengers clambered to get a better look. Gerard hung on tightly—occasionally smiling and waving to the curious passengers— as he fluttered from the wing like a kite on a string.

After a few minutes, he shouted down to Marty. "I don't know how much longer I can hang on, Marty. Can you do something?"

Marty looked around. There was a swimming pool right beside the bakery, so he ran over to the pool and shouted, "Everybody out!" He then brought the bins of flour from the bakery and unloaded them into the pool. "Okay, everybody back in. Knead that dough!" He ran down the street to the Rent-A-Dumptruck Company and rented the biggest truck they had, then raced off to the Booga Mega Market. "I need some yeast," he said breathlessly.

"We have two kinds," the clerk replied. "Regular, and fast-rising."

"I'll take the fast-rising," Marty gasped.

"And how much will you be needing?"

"I need enough to make one big loaf, and could you hurry please?"

"One pack should be enough then," the clerk said. Marty could see the clerk didn't understand what he meant by "big." Marty filled the whole truck with yeast, then headed back to the pool. He backed the truck up and emptied the yeast. As the yeast worked its way through the dough, Marty shouted, "Help is on the way, Gerard!"

The big mound of dough began to grow. It flowed over the swimming pool fence, rose above the bakery, and finally reached so high that it towered over Booga's tallest skyscraper.

Back in the sky, the pilot was still looping and twisting the plane, trying to shake Gerard. The pilot really wasn't paying attention to where he was going, and by the time he saw the dough it was too late. He plowed right into it. "Dough!" he said. Gerard fell off the plane and rolled safely down the pillowy dough, tumbling to a stop beside the bakery. The plane, however, disappeared into LoafLand.

"Thanks, Marty," Gerard said.

Over the next several days, Marty and Gerard began selling bits and pieces of the big loaf. Most of their customers were members of the search and rescue team, who were eating their way toward the plane. As it turned out, the plane passengers were also munching on the bread, trying to eat their way out. One week after the plane disappeared, the first plump passenger emerged from the loaf. "Hmmm boy!" he said. "That's the best bread I've ever tasted." Over the next few days, one by one, all the other missing passengers emerged from the big loaf.

When everyone was accounted for, the city of Booga held a big celebration. They feasted on bread sticks, bread pudding, and breaded banitski. It was a long day of festivities, and when Marty and Gerard finally got home, they were beat. As they jumped into their bunks, Marty commented, "Gerard, I was thinking. If yeast makes things grow, then if I ate enough I would be as tall as you, right?"

"Wrong, Marty. Yeast only works on dough, not on monkeys."

Marty plunked his head onto his pillow and sighed. "I guess I'll never be as tall as Gerard, except maybe in my dreams." On that thought, another glorious day in Booga Booga Land came to a close, and the two bushed bakers dozily drifted off to sleep.

The Parable of the Yeast

(Matthew 13:33)

The kingdom of heaven is like yeast that a woman took and mixed into a large amount of flour until it worked all through the dough.

In this short parable, there is an important truth regarding God's kingdom: God's kingdom is growing, and it will continue to grow until it has spread to every nation of the world. Quite simply, God's kingdom on earth is made up of His followers, people who have accepted the good news that Jesus came to save them from their sins.

So, when the parable talks about the yeast in the dough, it's saying that God's message will continue to be proclaimed around the world until every nation has had a chance to respond to it. If you have never responded to the good news that Jesus came to take away your sins and to make a way for you to get to heaven, then you can do that right now. Just ask Him to forgive you of your sins and to take control of your life. With this simple prayer you can begin a new journey—a journey that leads to your eternal home in heaven.

TEN
The Big Booga Bank

The birds were chirping in the nearby trees, and the sun was shining down on Marty as he stood on the high diving board looking at the shimmering water far below. The big loaf that once occupied the swimming pool was now gone, and life in Booga, the capital of Booga Booga Land, had returned to normal. Marty was getting ready to practice his Monkey Dive, a three somersaulter with a double twist. He sprang from the board, and as he spun in the air, he noticed a sign. On each revolution he read one word.

"Pool."

"Cleaning."

"Day."

He looked down. "Ooo boy." The pool plug had been pulled, and the water was going down faster than Marty. It wouldn't have been so bad had he done the three spins he had planned, but he did three and a half before hitting the bottom of the pool. He landed on his head. *Maybe I should get that helmet Gerard was talking about*, he thought as he picked himself up, then wobbled over to the bakery.

He was still rubbing his head when he saw Gerard. "Gerard, I have an idea. I was thinking we should sell the bakery and go into the banking business. What do you think?"

Gerard thought about the idea. Then he looked down at his little monkey friend. "Hmm, banking. We've been farmers and bakers, window washers and detectives, but we've never been bankers. Let's do it, Marty!" The next day they sold their bakery. Soon after, their new bank, the Big Booga Bank, opened for business.

The Big Booga Bank was an architectural splendor, with eighteen-foot-high decorated doors and ornate eighteen-foot ceilings. Marty appointed himself chief of security, while Gerard happily took on the role of bank manager. Being the head of security, Marty made his tough policies known right from the start. When the first customer walked into the bank, Marty dropped from the ceiling and landed on him. "You're not going to rob this bank!" Marty said as he wrestled the man to the floor.

The customer explained he was just coming in to use the pop machine. Marty apologized. Then he helped the man back to his feet.

About an hour later, the same man reentered the bank. He looked up at the ceiling, then from side to side. Marty was nowhere to be seen, and the man breathed a sigh of relief. Just then Marty came bolting out of a closet. He had been hiding there, and he was now ready to deliver the Wookee Hookee, a maneuver designed to disable thieves. Marty jumped high into the air and soared toward the man, preparing to deliver the wallop. The man ducked, and Marty flew over the man's head and slammed into a wall. *Oookay, I wasn't expecting that*, Marty thought as he dropped to the floor. The man looked at Marty apprehensively. Then he made his way over to Gerard.

"Sorry about the monkey," Gerard said as he looked at the customer. "Now, can I help you with something?"

"Yes. My name is Bo, and I was wondering if I could borrow some money."

"Okay, and how much can we set you up with, Bo?"

"Uh, I'd like five hundred thousand bamolies, please."

Gerard leaned back in his chair as he considered the man's request. They had a lot of money in their vault, and lending a half million bamolies would not be a problem. "Okay, Bo," Gerard said.

"Marty, could you please pull five hundred thousand bamolies from the vault for this fine gentleman?"

Marty went over to the vault and started dialing in the combination. "41 – 59 . . . or was it 59 – 41 . . . ?" He couldn't remember.

Fortunately, he had it written down—somewhere. He called Gerard over. "Gerard, do you remember where I put the combination?"

"Marty, you wouldn't tell me anything. Remember, you said the chief of security couldn't take any chances."

"Right. Oh, I know! I put it on the bottom of my shoe." Marty looked at his shoe, but the numbers were clean gone. "Uh, Gerard, you haven't seen some numbers stamped on the floor anywhere, have you?"

Just then Bo called out from the other room, "Is there a problem?"

"Don't worry, Gerard," Marty said. "I'll think of something. You just go back and take care of Bo."

As Gerard returned to his office, Marty pulled out the custom, cordless Holtmeister rock-coring drill. Gerard could feel the hair on his mane straighten as Marty began drilling a hole in the vault wall. Gerard shuddered at the thought of what was going to happen next. There was an eerie silence, then a thunderous explosion.

BOOM! This was followed by a THUD! and a loud "OUCH!" as Marty was catapulted into the air and landed on the sidewalk outside of the bank. Marty staggered over to Bo, covered in dirt and dust.

"Here's your money, Bo. Repayment is due in one year."

A year later, on payback day, Bo returned to the bank.

Bo started off with some bad news. "Gerard, I can't repay the loan. I blew all of your bamolies on bingo."

Gerard cleared his throat. "Uh, Bo, I'm not quite sure I heard what you said. How would you like to try repeating that?"

"Look, Gerard, I'm really sorry. I've already enrolled in bingo reform school, and I'm going to repay your loan as soon as I can. Will you give me a chance, please?"

Marty was standing close by, and he overheard the conversation. He motioned for Gerard to come into the hallway. After a short discussion, Gerard returned to his office. "Bo, Marty has convinced me to show a little mercy here, and we've decided to give you a break. You don't have to repay the loan." With that announcement, Gerard ripped up Bo's loan agreement.

Bo was ecstatic. He profusely thanked Marty and Gerard. Then he walked out of the bank. "Party time!" he shouted. He pulled out his wallet and looked inside. It was empty. "Oookay, forget the party."

As he walked down the street, Bo spotted an old bingo buddy.

Bo's mood suddenly changed. His buddy owed him two bamolies, and Bo confronted him.

"Give me my two bamolies!" Bo demanded.

His buddy was broke.

"If you don't give me my two bamolies, I'm going to send you to the klinker!"

His buddy begged for mercy, but Bo had no mercy to give. The Booga police were called in, but they had a hard time figuring out what to do. Finally, someone suggested that Marty and Gerard be informed, and Bo was taken to the bank. When Bo arrived, Gerard was not smiling, and neither was Marty. "What do you have to say for yourself, Bo?"

Bo was silent.

"Bo, do you remember that loan agreement we tore up?" Marty asked.

Bo nodded.

"Well, we kept a copy. And now do you know what my giraffe friend and I are going to do?"

Bo shook his head.

"Bo, we've arranged a trip for you, one way, to the island of Losta Sola." Marty gave Bo a briefcase with his ticket, then Bo walked out the door. As Bo wondered why he needed such a big briefcase for one measly ticket—and why it was so heavy—Marty and Gerard began the countdown. "Three, two, one . . ." KABOOOM!! Bo's "ticket" was a pack of Kapowee rods, and he was now sailing through the air on his way to Losta Sola.

That night, as Marty and Gerard sat around the supper table, Marty commented, "Gerard, Bo's problem was more than just money, wasn't it?"

"That's right, Marty. I think the vault of his heart was as empty as his wallet."

After supper, Marty and Gerard jumped right into their bunks. Gerard turned out the lights, and, in a banker's blink, the little monkey and the tall giraffe were on their way to Snooza Snooza Land.

The Parable of the Unmerciful Servant

(Matthew 18:23-35)

Therefore, the kingdom of heaven is like a king who wanted to settle accounts with his servants. As he began the settlement, a man who owed him ten thousand talents was brought to him. Since he was not able to pay, the master ordered that he and his wife and his children and all that he had be sold to repay the debt.

The servant fell on his knees before him. "Be patient with me," he begged, "and I will pay back everything."

The servant's master took pity on him, canceled the debt, and let him go.

But when that servant went out, he found one of his fellow servants who owed him a hundred denarii. He grabbed him and began to choke him. "Pay back what you owe me!" he demanded.

His fellow servant fell to his knees and begged him, "Be patient with me, and I will pay you back."

But he refused. Instead, he went off and had the man thrown into prison until he could pay the debt. When the other servants saw what had happened, they were greatly distressed and went and told their master everything that had happened.

Then the master called the servant in. "You wicked servant," he said, "I canceled all that debt of yours because you begged me to. Shouldn't you have had mercy on your fellow servant just as I had on you?" In anger his master turned him over to the jailers to be tortured, until he should pay back all he owed.

This is how my heavenly Father will treat each of you unless you forgive your brother from your heart.

In this parable, Jesus is saying that people who have experienced the forgiveness of God should in turn offer forgiveness to others. The debt the servant owed his master was huge, and it is a picture of the huge debt that everyone who sins owes to God. Sin carries with it a penalty, and that penalty is eternal death. Without God's help—that is, without God cancelling that debt—everyone would be doomed.

The good news is: God *has* sent help. He sent His Son to die on a cross to forgive us of our sins, and if we accept His forgiveness, we are freed from the death penalty and given eternal life. God's forgiveness is huge, and we need to realize that. This parable is teaching us that we should be so grateful to God for what He has done for us that we are motivated to willingly forgive others, regardless of how badly they have wronged us.

ELEVEN
The Duet Brothers

It was a splendid summer morning in Booga, the capital of Booga Booga Land, and the sun was shining brightly through Marty and Gerard's bedroom window. Although it was mid-morning, they were both still sound asleep, and Gerard was snoring. His snoring began getting louder, until finally it became so loud that Marty's bunk began to shake. Marty rocked from one side of his bunk to the other, coming dangerously close to rolling off. Gerard gave one big blast, and Marty rolled over the edge, tumbled through the air, and landed on the floor. Gerard was awakened by the THUMP! and drowsily looked down at Marty. Marty slowly rose to his feet, then looked up at the big giraffe. "Gerard, I was thinking about something . . ."

"I know," Gerard yawned. "Sideboards on your bunk, right?"

"No . . . I was thinking we should sell the bank and become electricians."

Gerard thought about the idea. He was still a wee bit sleepy and wasn't quite sure if Marty's idea was a good one, but by the time Gerard fully awoke, Marty had sold the bank and enrolled himself and Gerard in Eddy's Electrical Institute of Technology.

On day one of classes, Marty and Gerard took their seats and listened to Eddy as he lectured on Ohm's Law, Cole's Law, and Eddy currents. Cole slaw was sounding pretty good to Gerard, as it was getting pretty close to lunchtime. None of the laws were sounding good to Marty, as he was falling asleep. Before dozing off, though, Marty had hooked up a shock device to give him an electric jolt, in the event he fell asleep and the teacher called out his name. It wasn't long before his device was tested.

"Marty," Eddy said. The device kicked in and Marty bolted to an upright position. "Yes, sir!"

"Marty," Eddy continued. Marty was jolted again. *Oooo, maybe this wasn't such a good idea*, he thought.

"Is there something wrong, Marty?"

"Oooo . . . uh, no, sir," Marty said as he struggled with the device, trying to shut it off.

"I was wondering if you could tell the class how Kirchoff's Law applies to phasors in a split capacitance motor?"

Ooo boy . . . Marty thought. "Well, sir . . ." He opened his textbook at random and began reading. "It determines the capacitor's impedance in the resonant circuit at varying phase voltages . . . I hope."

"Very good, Marty."

"Duh!" Marty got zapped again. He ripped the wires out of the shock device and decided he would just stay awake for the rest of the class.

After sitting through a week of lectures, it was finally time for Marty and Gerard to begin hands-on training. Eddy was standing at the front of the classroom displaying a broken toaster when Marty jumped up and said, "I know how to fix those things, sir."

He ran to the front of the classroom and was just about to stick a knife in when Eddy said, "Uh, Marty . . ." Marty looked up at Eddy.

"It's okay, Eddy. I've done this at home lots of times." Marty stuck the knife in and promptly received a massive electric shock. He popped into the air and flew across the room, smoking like a burnt piece of toast. "Of course, I've never tried it with the toaster plugged in before . . ." Marty said as he picked himself up, then staggered back to his seat.

Following a few more lessons, Eddy came to the topic of power-pole installations. As it turned out, this was Marty and Gerard's favorite section. Gerard finally got to work at a height suitable for him, and Marty got to operate a lift truck. Every time Marty jumped into the bucket, he would buzz up and down, going everywhere except where he was supposed to. Eddy had to remind Marty that the bucket was to be used just to get to the top of the pole; it was not an amusement-park ride.

Eventually Marty and Gerard graduated, and, being entrepreneurs, they decided to open their own business. There were a lot of fruit growers in the Booga area, and they were having problems with a pesky little bug called the Koojikowa. Marty thought about the problem, then, remembering the toaster incident, he came up with an idea. "Gerard, let's make zappers!"

The next day, Marty and Gerard opened up an electrical shop and began building bug zappers. It didn't take long for their business to start booming, and soon there was just too much work for them to handle. They decided to hire two more electricians, and after interviewing several candidates, they decided to hire the Duet brothers.

Marty took on the task of training the brothers, while Gerard went into the field to install the zappers. Marty first showed the brothers around the shop and then gave each of them a simple task to do. He asked the first brother, Iwill, to fix the particle accelerator on the shop's lawn mower. Marty then asked Iwill's brother, Iwohnt, to fix the photon sensor on the shop's vacuum cleaner.

Iwill said he would have the lawnmower fixed before lunch. But Iwohnt told Marty he wouldn't touch the vacuum cleaner, and that he was going on strike for higher wages. As Marty thought about what to do, he told Iwohnt that the matter would have to be discussed with Gerard. Marty left the two brothers in the shop. Then he went to the fruit field where Gerard was working.

Gerard was halfway through installing a bug zapper when he saw Marty coming. "Marty, could you give me a hand up here, please?"

Marty was distracted by a Koojikowa and hadn't heard Gerard. Gerard looked down at Marty. "Yo, Marty! I could use a little help up here!"

Marty threw a banana peel at the pesky little bug. Then he began the long climb up the eighteen-foot-tall giraffe. Marty was just about at Gerard's head when the big giraffe stepped on the banana peel and fell to the ground. Marty quickly grabbed onto a bug zapper. That was a mistake he wouldn't soon forget. He received a massive shock, then let go. That was another mistake. Marty tumbled through the air and landed on the hard ground right beside Gerard. He picked himself up and looked up at Gerard. "Gerard, I have a problem."

"You're not the only one, Marty."

"No, I mean I have a problem back at the shop with Iwohnt. He said he won't fix the vacuum cleaner and that he wants to go on strike." After Marty had given Gerard the details, they decided to head back to the shop to see what they could do.

When they arrived, Iwohnt was sitting outside on the steps eating his lunch. Much to Marty and Gerard's surprise, he had already fixed the vacuum cleaner. The problem now was with Iwill; he hadn't even started working on the lawn mower.

Over the next several weeks, Iwill continued to make promises that he never kept. However, Iwohnt continued to help out, even in the times he said he wouldn't. Marty and Gerard eventually called a meeting and had the two brothers come into their office.

"Iwohnt," Marty began, "you've done a lot of work around here, and, although your attitude needs a little polish, Gerard and I have decided to give you that raise you've been asking for."

Marty then turned to Iwill. "Iwill, you're going to be getting something too."

"Oh boy!" Iwill said excitedly.

"You're getting fired."

"Ooo . . . what a downer."

Iwohnt thanked Marty and Gerard and then skipped out of their office on his way to Monty's Malt and Milkshake Shop for a banana-split celebration. Iwill, on the other hand, was feeling a little more like a split banana as he shuffled out of their office and headed for the soup kitchen. That night when Marty and Gerard arrived home, they sat down at the supper table and dug into a double-thick coconut cream pie. They then headed for their bunks, and as Marty was turning out the lights, he commented, "Gerard, I think Iwill and Iwohnt should swap names. What do you think?"

"Mmff," Gerard replied. Marty peeked over the edge of his bunk. "Gerard, was that a 'Yes' mmff or a 'No' mmff?"

There was no reply.

I guess it was a "Yes" mmff, Marty thought as he tucked himself in and rolled over. Soon the on-again, off-again snores of the two tired electricians were the only thing heard, as the little monkey and the big giraffe serenely drifted off to Snooza Snooza Land.

The Parable of the Two Sons

(Matthew 21:28-31)

"There was a man who had two sons. He went to the first and said, 'Son, go and work today in the vineyard.'

'I will not,' he answered, but later he changed his mind and went.

"Then the father went to the other son and said the same thing. He answered, 'I will, sir,' but he did not go.

"Which of the two did what his father wanted?"

"The first," they answered.

In this parable, Jesus is talking about repentance and the importance it has on our relationship with God. You see, sin messes up our relationship with God, and we need to get rid of that sin through repentance. The father who asked his sons to go and work in his vineyard really represents God asking people to repent of their sins. Some say, "I will," and some say, "I won't." God wants to have a relationship with us. He wants us to trust Him and to be committed to Him, and He is looking for heartfelt repentance, not just words. Saying "I will" is not enough. We must follow up our words with actions, for it is by our actions—that is, by the way we live our daily lives—that we show God how much we love Him and are committed to Him.

TWELVE
Clothes by Marty

The sun was shining brightly over Booga, the capital of Booga Booga Land, as Marty hopped on his three-wheeler and Gerard laced up his track shoes. It was the end of another workday and they were preparing to race home. There was a slice of coconut cream pie in the fridge awaiting the winner.

"The pie's mine," Marty said as he shot into the lead, weaving in and out of people, power poles, and parking meters. Gerard quickly came up from behind, though, and his long legs propelled him past Marty. Neither one stopped as they approached a busy intersection. Gerard tiptoed over the cars, while Marty jumped his trike. "Going up!" he said as he flew into the air and over the intersection. Unfortunately, there was a power pole on the other side.

"Going down," he said as he hit the pole. Marty picked himself up and pushed his wobbly tricycle the rest of the way home. He arrived just in time to see Gerard finish off the pie.

"You know, Gerard, if it wasn't for that pole, I would have easily beaten you." Marty pushed his tricycle across the kitchen floor, then put it into the garburator.

"I'm sure you would have," Gerard said. "Just like I'm sure the garburator would still be working if you hadn't put your tricycle in it." Marty looked into the kitchen sink. The garburator had ground to a halt. As Marty tried to unjam it, he looked up at Gerard. "Gerard, I have an idea."

"I know. You're going to call a plumber, right?"

"No . . . I was thinking we should go into a new line of business. What do you think about us taking up tailoring?"

Gerard thought about the idea. The idea of tailoring suited him just fine, so the next day they sold their electrical shop and opened up a tailoring company.

Marty painted a sign for their new company and proudly displayed it outside of their shop. The sign read Clothes by Marty.

Gerard looked at the sign and then looked down at Marty. "Marty, unless you plan on stitching up all of the clothes by yourself, you'd better change that sign." The next day their store reopened under the name Clothes by Marty *and* Gerard.

The first customer to walk through their doors was the chief of Booga's police force. "I need fifty uniforms for my men," he said. "The president is going to inspect my troops next week, and I need my men looking smart."

"We'll make them look smart, sir," Marty assured the chief.

As the chief walked out the door, Gerard looked over at Marty. "Uh, Marty, making the Booga police force look smart isn't going to be all that easy, you know."

Marty was up for the challenge, though, and he immediately began working on the uniforms. He came up with a design. Then he handed the fabric over to Gerard for stitching. Gerard looked at the outdated powder-blue polyester fabric and shook his head. *I wonder what the chief is going to think when he sees these things*, he thought.

One day before the inspection, the chief came in to pick up the uniforms. He looked at the uniforms, paused for a moment, then smiled contentedly. "The president has some misgivings regarding the competency of my troops, but with these new uniforms, I'm sure all of his doubts will be erased."

Let's hope so, Gerard thought as he packaged the uniforms, then handed them to the chief.

The inspection was to be a public affair, taking on the form of a parade through the streets of Booga. Two hours before inspection time, the police were given their new uniforms. To their surprise, the jacket sleeves were twice as long as their arms and the pants barely covered their knees. The chief assured his troops that the uniforms were the latest craze in fashion and that the president was sure to be impressed.

Large crowds began gathering along the streets of Booga, and by the time the procession started, the streets were full. As the chief and his troops strutted down Booga's main street decked out in their powder-blue polyester knickerbockers and floppy-sleeved jackets, the onlooking crowd didn't know whether to laugh or cry.

Most laughed so hard that they began to cry. The president was laughing too. All doubts regarding the competency of his police force were erased. He was now convinced they were incompetent.

After the parade, Marty and Gerard's tailoring business began to boom. Parade-goers had never seen such imaginative uniforms, and customers from all across the country began coming to their shop. One day, even the president's daughter, Betty, came in for a visit. She was wearing a leopard-skin jacket and was carrying a lovely wool sweater, along with her cat, Snickers.

"Sweet little Snickers accidentally tore a hole in my favorite sweater," Betty explained. "Can you fix it?"

"No problem," Marty said. "Give us a week and we'll have it looking as good as new."

As she was walking out the door, another pair of unexpected customers came in: Stan and his shaggy dog, Rufus. Unfortunately, Rufus saw Snickers, and that was the beginning of chaos. Rufus jumped at Snickers, then Snickers jumped from Betty's arms. Unfortunately, Snickers ripped a hole in Betty's leopard-skin jacket.

"Don't worry, Betty. We can fix it," Marty said.

Unfortunately, when Rufus jumped, he missed Snickers and landed on Betty, ripping another hole in her jacket.

"No extra charge for that one," Marty said. Rufus then bounded out the door in pursuit of Snickers.

"And what can we do for you, Stan?" Marty asked after the mayhem had moved outdoors. Stan was wearing an old leather jacket riddled with holes. "Rufus got at it," he explained.

"We'll have it looking like new in a week," Marty assured him.

Just then Rufus came back into the store, out of breath.

"Where's the cat, Rufus?" Stan asked.

"Woof," Rufus barked, dog talk for "She's on a power pole, ten blocks away."

Gerard volunteered to go rescue Snickers, while Stan apologized to Betty for Rufus's mischievous behavior.

One week later, Stan and Betty came in to pick up their garments. Stan's jacket was repaired and looking like new, as was Betty's wool sweater. The leopard-skin jacket, however, was still not mended.

"We're having a few problems finding a leopard," Marty explained.

Another week passed by, and the leopard-skin jacket still hadn't been repaired. What's more, Betty, Stan, and Rufus returned for a surprise visit. Betty put her sweater on the counter, Stan put his jacket on the counter, and Rufus put his paws on the counter.

"What brings you folks back so soon?" Marty asked as he pulled out a doggy biscuit for Rufus.

"We washed these clothes, and your patches shrunk. The holes are bigger now than they were before!"

Marty inspected the garments. "Well, paint me white and call me a polar bear! I guess new material just doesn't work on old clothes." Marty looked over at Gerard, then handed him the clothes for mending. "Gerard will have these clothes fixed in a jiffy." Gerard wasn't quite so optimistic, but he took the garments anyway and got right to work.

Betty then asked, "And how's my leopard-skin jacket coming?"

"Uh, well . . ." Marty looked out the window. A leopard just happened to be passing by. "Just give me a minute, Betty. Rufus, there's a cat . . ." The words were barely out of Marty's mouth when Rufus bounded out the door. There was a clatter, followed by a hissing sound and a snarl. Then Rufus returned to the shop. He had a few scratches on his nose.

"Did you get the cat, Rufus?" Marty asked.

Rufus shook his head.

"Did the cat get you?"

Rufus nodded.

Marty turned to Betty. "Uh, is it okay if we use imitation leopard skin?" She agreed, and that night Marty and Gerard worked extra hard to finish the garments. They used old leather, old wool, and non-shrinkable fake leopard skin. They finished mending the garments in the wee hours of the morning and then sent them by Wookawooni Express to their owners.

When Marty and Gerard finally got home, they were exhausted. There were two slices of banana cream pie left in the fridge, and Marty ate them both. Gerard looked down at Marty.

Marty looked up at Gerard.

"Sorry, Gerard. You can have my box of Coconut Crispies," Marty said as he tried to patch up the situation. Gerard checked the Coconut Crispy box. It was empty.

I guess that hole just got bigger, Marty thought.

"It's okay, Marty. I'll just chew on some leaves."

As they were hopping into their bunks, Marty reflected, *That Gerard sure knows how to patch up holes.* He then snuggled under his covers, and in a tailor's stitch, the big giraffe and the little monkey were on their way to Snooza Snooza Land.

The Parable of the Patched Garment

(Mark 2:21)

No one sews a patch of unshrunk cloth on an old garment. If he does, the new piece will pull away from the old, making the tear worse.

This parable is talking about Jesus and how He came to bring renewal to the hearts and lives of people. His teachings and His way of doing things were very different than the religious practices of His day. Just like the unshrunk cloth was not suitable for patching up old clothes, Jesus' teachings were not meant to patch up the religious practices of His day. They were meant to change them. Jesus showed us that God does not want us to relate to Him by just going through the motions of following rules or traditions. Rather, He wants us to love Him, to talk to Him, and to walk with Him, just as in a personal relationship. That's what Jesus demonstrated when He was here on earth, and that is the example God wants us to follow.

THIRTEEN
The 3P2C

The sun was on its way to Booga, the capital of Booga Booga Land, and in just a few hours it would be ushering in a new day. Marty and Gerard were in no hurry to get up, and if the sun were to put off its arrival, they'd be just as happy. Marty was in the middle of an action-packed dream and he was tossing and turning as the action intensified, then BAM! He was hit by an idea. He woke up and crawled down from his bunk, being careful to not disturb Gerard. Marty reset Gerard's alarm clock, then waited . . . BZZZZZ! Gerard jumped up, hit the alarm, then looked outside. It was still dark. He plunked his head back onto his pillow, then sighed, "What is it this time, Marty?"

Marty peeked out from under Gerard's bunk. "Gerard, I was thinking we should become vacuum-cleaner salesmen."

As Gerard poured himself a glass of milk for breakfast, he thought about the idea. "Marty, and just where are we going to get the vacuum cleaners from?"

"We'll make them, Gerard."

The next day they opened a research and development branch in their tailoring shop, and after two months of hard work, they had their first model built. They asked one of their customers to try it out for a day, then to report back regarding its performance.

The chief of Booga's police force volunteered to test the unit. The chief decided to test the vacuum cleaner on the day he was to make an important presentation to the president of Booga Booga Land. The chief took the vacuum along thinking he would clean his suit just before he went into the meeting. As the chief was standing outside of the president's door, he fired up the vacuum cleaner and began cleaning his powder-blue polyester uniform.

The vacuum was so powerful that it swallowed his jacket. Startled, the chief dropped the vacuum hose, only to have the vacuum pilfer his shoes and socks too! The meeting was a memorable one, and it certainly left an impression on the president. After the meeting, the barefooted chief returned to the tailoring shop.

"A little too much power there, eh, chief?" Marty remarked as he assessed the chief's looks. "I guess Gerard was right. I really shouldn't have put that supercharger on the motor."

Over the next several months, Marty and Gerard worked diligently on developing another model, a model specifically designed for clothes cleaning. They worked through prototype after prototype, and finally came up with a pocket-sized model that performed magnificently. They called it the "Professional Portable Personal Clothes Cleaner," also known as the "3P2C." They developed a sales strategy, then decided to travel across the country to promote their new product.

Before setting out on their journey, though, they hired three door-to-door salesmen: Mutch Sellzalot, Sammy Sellzem, and Stuey Storzit. Marty explained to the three salesmen, "Gerard and I will be gone for three months, and during our absence we are counting on you to sell vacuum cleaners in Booga. Each of you is expected to meet a quota, based on your experience. Mutch, you will have to sell ten units. Sammy, you will have to sell five. And Stuey, you only have to sell one." After giving the salesmen these instructions, Marty and Gerard packed their bags, then left Booga.

The salesmen wasted no time in getting to work. Mutch headed out right away and made an appointment with Bob, the president of Booga Booga Land. Sammy also got a fast start, as he contacted the office of the chief of Booga's police force. Stuey was a little slow, though, and he just hung around the shop, not really sure what to do.

During Mutch's meeting with Bob, Mutch noticed a few chocolate cake crumbs on Bob's suit jacket. Mutch demonstrated the effectiveness of the 3P2C to remove the crumbs. Then he gave Bob a recipe for crumbless chocolate cake. Bob was very impressed, and he bought five units right there on the spot. As Mutch was leaving the building, he sold his remaining units to each person he met: Bob's secretary, the cleaning lady, the cafeteria cook, a man talking on a pay phone, and the door porter.

At the office of the chief of police, Sammy was also hard at work. He knew this might be a tough sell, but his name wasn't Sammy Sellzem for nothing. As expected, the chief was a bit reluctant to try the new clothes cleaner, but Sammy had a few tricks up his sleeve. After showing the chief the 3P2C's ability to clean all fabrics safely—including powder-blue polyester—Sammy sweetened the pot by throwing in an accessory to create Einstein hair.

Now the chief was listening. He had always wanted Einstein hair, and it just might improve his chances of impressing the president too. Sammy didn't stop at that, though. If the chief bought two or more units, he would also receive a special nozzle to clean donut crumbs from police cruisers.

"Now about the cost, Sammy," the chief said. "Are these things going to clean the money right out of my pockets?"

"That's a good one, Chief," Sammy said smoothly. "Actually, I'm going to cut you a deal. One unit normally sells for thirty-nine bamolies, but I'm willing to sell you five for only two hundred and fifty."

"Wait a minute . . ." the chief said calculatingly. "Do I still get the donut crumb nozzle?"

Sammy sighed. "For sure, Chief, and that'll save you another thirty bamolies!"

"Sounds like a good deal to me, Sammy," the chief said. "I'll take all five."

While Sammy and Mutch were meeting their quotas, Stuey was

still at the shop trying to figure out what to do. *Maybe my mom will buy one*, he thought. *Then again, I'd have to wait until she visited.*

He went outside and sat on the steps. He watched as an old man passed by, walking his dog. Stuey never thought of asking the man if he wanted to buy a 3P2C. A lady carrying a cat then walked by. Stuey didn't ask her either. A short time later a dog chasing a cat zoomed by. Stuey didn't say a word as the old man passed by again shouting after his dog, "Come back here, Rufus!" As Stuey sat there wondering what to do, he decided just to store the unit. That way it would be as good as new when Marty and Gerard returned.

Time passed and, at the end of three months, Marty and Gerard came back to Booga. They immediately called the salesmen together and asked each one of them to report on how many units they had sold. Mutch reported he had sold all ten of his units, Sammy reported he sold his five, and Stuey reported that his mom never visited. He returned his one unit to Marty and Gerard.

"Alrighty then," Marty said as he stood up to address the salesmen. "Gerard and I have decided to reward each of you with a little something for your efforts. Mutch, you will be promoted to manager of sales. Sammy, you are hereby promoted to manager of marketing, and Stuey . . . well, Stuey, for returning the one unit you were supposed to sell, Gerard and I have created the 'Stuey Storzit Memorial Award.' Here's a briefcase with a one-way ticket to Losta Sola." Stuey was given a fine leather briefcase, then escorted to the door.

As Stuey walked out the door with the heavy briefcase, Marty and Gerard began the countdown: "Three, two, one . . ." KABOOOM!! Stuey was on his way across the ocean to the island of Losta Sola.

Business is tough sometimes, Marty and Gerard thought as they walked home that night, tired from their trip and the events of the day. When they arrived home, they cooked up a dish of leaf lasagna and pulled out two thick slices of coconut cream pie. After supper, they jumped into their vacuum-cleaned jammies, and it was lights out. Soon, only muffled snores were heard, as the two sleepy salesmen sailed serenely off to Snooza Snooza Land.

The Parable of the Talents

(Matthew 25:14-30)

Again, it will be like a man going on a journey, who called his servants and entrusted his property to them. To one he gave five talents of money, to another two talents, and to another one talent, each according to his ability.

Then he went on his journey. The man who had received the five talents went at once and put his money to work and gained five more. So also, the one with the two talents gained two more. But the man who had received the one talent went off, dug a hole in the ground and hid his master's money.

After a long time the master of those servants returned and settled accounts with them. The man who had received the five talents brought the other five.

"Master," he said, "you entrusted me with five talents. See, I have gained five more."

His master replied, "Well done, good and faithful servant! You have been faithful with a few things; I will put you in charge of many things. Come and share your master's happiness!"

The man with the two talents also came. "Master," he said, "you entrusted me with two talents; see, I have gained two more."

His master replied, "Well done, good and faithful servant! You have been faithful with a few things; I will put you in charge of many things. Come and share your master's happiness!"

Then the man who had received the one talent came. "Master," he said, "I knew that you are a hard man, harvesting where you have not sown and gathering where you have not scattered seed. So I was afraid and went out and hid your talent in the ground. See, here is what belongs to you."

His master replied, "You wicked, lazy servant! So you knew that I harvest where I have not sown and gather where I have not scattered seed? Well then, you should have put my money on deposit with the bankers, so that when I returned I would have received it back with interest.

"Take the talent from him and give it to the one who has the ten talents. For everyone who has will be given more, and he will have an abundance. Whoever does not have, even what he has will be taken from him. And throw that worthless servant outside, into the darkness, where there will be weeping and gnashing of teeth."

In this parable Jesus is saying that His followers have been given a job to do and that when He returns to earth they will be evaluated for their efforts. The two servants who managed their master's money well—like the hardworking Mutch and Sammy—represent people with whom Jesus will be pleased. The lazy servant—like Stuey—represents someone who is going to be in trouble. God has given people certain abilities to be used to strengthen and expand His kingdom, and He wants His people to use them well. So, if He's given you the ability to teach, then do it enthusiastically and teach people about Him until you get hand cramps. If He's given you the ability to preach, then tell people about God until they have to lock you up. And if He's given you the ability to encourage, then visit people in the hospital until they get sick of seeing you. Above all, don't be idle. For just like Stuey, deep sorrow awaits those who have been given a job to do yet, because they are lazy, just sit around and do nothing.

FOURTEEN
WannawaWHAT?

The radiant blue sky above Booga Booga Land looked like an ocean to Marty, as he hung upside down on the monkey bars in Booga Park. He was waiting for Gerard to return from Monty's Malt and Milkshake Shop with a couple of creamy vanilla twisters. Marty had been practicing a new dismount, and when he spotted Gerard coming in the distance, he prepared for a little razzle-dazzle. Marty grabbed the bar with his feet, then began swinging around and around. He soon was swinging so fast that he didn't know which way was up or which way was down.

Gerard's really going to be impressed with this move! Marty thought as he let go of the bar. Unfortunately, he let go at the bottom of his swing and shot headfirst into the dirt.

"Drilling for oil, or just doing a soil hardness test?" Gerard asked as Marty got up and shook the dirt from his ears. Marty looked up at Gerard. "Gerard, I really think we need a holiday." Gerard gave Marty a creamy vanilla twister, then thought about the idea. They hadn't taken a holiday since coming to Booga, and they both could use a little bit of a break. So Gerard agreed. The very next day they sold their tailoring shop, along with all of their 3P2C vacuum cleaners, then bought a dump truck and prepared to go on vacation.

Marty excitedly jumped behind the wheel of the truck, then buckled himself in. "Wannawaheenee, here we come!"

"Wannawawhat?" Gerard said as he jumped into the back of the truck, then braced himself as best he could. Marty didn't reply; he just put the pedal to the metal, and they were off.

Marty wasn't one for staying on the road, and he soon had the truck going in and out of ditches and across fields. When he finally pulled the truck into Wannawaheenee, he sped down the beach, slaloming around people, hot dog stands, and popsicle carts. After creating a sandstorm, he brought the truck to a stop and jumped out. "Hey, Gerard, we're here! Gerard?" Four hours later Gerard came running down the beach, out of breath. He had fallen out of the truck back at Booga.

They decided to camp right where Marty had stopped the truck, and they soon had their tent up and their beach towels down. "Now for a little music," Marty said as he pulled out his radio. Unfortunately, when he turned it on, there was no sound. He shook it, fidgeted with all the buttons, then shook it again. There was still no sound.

He was just about to throw it away, when Gerard suggested, "Uh, Marty, you did put batteries in it, right?"

"Gerard, you'd have to be a little bit loopy to forget something like that. Know what I mean?" Marty opened the battery compartment. It was empty. Gerard looked down at Marty.

"Look, Gerard, I'm sure I put batteries in there."

Marty wasn't about to give up now, and he soon came up with another idea to get power to his radio. "Gerard, could you give me a hand with this extension cord, please?" Marty pulled out a long extension cord, and together they dragged it across the beach to a nearby hotel. As Gerard went back to the beach, Marty began looking for a plug-in. Unfortunately, all of the sockets were full. *I don't think anybody is using this one*, Marty thought as he pulled out someone's cord and plugged in his own. As he was walking back to the beach, Marty heard a big THUD! He turned on his radio just in time to hear the news of a window washer who had fallen from his platform, after it had lost power. *Hmm*, Marty thought, *I wonder how that happened?*

At their campsite that night, Marty lit a big bonfire, then began roasting marshmallows. Gerard was sitting by the beach enjoying the sunset when an errant marshmallow hit him on the nose.

Marty was flinging marshmallows at the truck. Gerard looked at Marty, then licked the marshmallow off of his nose. He returned his attention to the bay. "Marty, do you see anything out there?"

Marty strained his eyes. The water was rippling in the distance, and it looked like someone was trying to swim to shore. A short time later, a man dragged himself onto the beach, exhausted and hungry.

"Would you like a marshmallow?" Marty offered.

"I'd be grateful for anything right now," the man said as he huddled close to the fire. Marty picked a few freshly roasted marshmallows off of the truck and gave them to the stranger. The weary man explained, "My name is Slim Pickens, and I've been out there swimming for three days. I have come from the Land of Little, and I'm looking for my brother, Slam." As he was talking, a man on crutches hobbled by.

"Slam!" Slim shouted.

"Slim?" Slam, Slim's brother, said.

"Slam, it's so good to see you. What happened to you?"

"Someone unplugged my window-washing platform this afternoon," he said as he limped over to the fire. There were a lot of interesting stories shared around the campfire that night, and it was late in the evening when Slim and Slam finally said their good-byes and went on their way.

The next morning, Marty and Gerard were out for a stroll checking out the town when they heard a ruckus coming from a nearby restaurant. They looked across the street and saw two raggedly clothed men come flying out of the restaurant's front door. A hefty, stern-looking man stood at the door, clapping dust from his hands. Marty and Gerard went over and discovered the men were from Slim and Slam's home country, the Land of Little.

The men were too poor to buy anything for themselves, and they were just looking for a few scraps of food. Gerard stuck his head in the restaurant door and ordered up two pizzas for the ragmen, while Marty pulled out a few roasted marshmallows. While in the restaurant, Gerard discovered the owner was a mean man named Sid Snort. He owned most of the hotels and restaurants in Wannawaheenee, and he was notoriously unkind to people from the Land of Little.

The next day as Marty and Gerard were out walking, they again noticed Sid Snort. He walked up to a poor panhandler and kicked his pan clear across the street. Marty and Gerard hurried over and helped the panhandler gather his few coins, then gave him a crisp hundred-bamoly bill. Sid continued walking on down the street and eventually went into one of his hotels. At the entrance to his hotel was a sign: "No Vacancy (if you're from the Land of Little)." Sid was a meany through and through.

Several weeks passed, and Marty and Gerard continued to help people from the Land of Little. Then a very strange thing happened. One day a huge ocean liner pulled into Wannawaheenee. The captain of the ship was a king from a faraway country called Gloryland. Unknown to the residents, this king had bought Wannawaheenee, and he now owned everything.

When he discovered the mistreatment of the Land of Little people by Sid Snort and the kindness of Marty and Gerard, the king took immediate action. He gave all of Sid's hotels and restaurants to Marty and Gerard. Then he took Mr. Snort on board the ship.

This isn't such a bad deal, Sid thought as he waved good-bye to the Wannawaheenians, then set sail for Gloryland. Along the way, though, the ocean liner passed by Losta Sola. To Sid's surprise, he was unceremoniously dumped on the isolated island, then left abandoned.

That night Marty and Gerard held a big celebration party in honor of all the Land of Little people. All of Wannawaheenee was invited to the feast. They dined on juicy barbecued Banooki burgers; thick, mouth-watering steakasaurus; and tantalizing tropical truffle. The festivities went well into the night, and by the time Marty and Gerard returned to their beach camp, they were bushed. They plopped into their sleeping bags, and, in the flip of a burger, they were off to Snooza Snooza Land.

The Parable of the Sheep and the Goats
(Matthew 25:31-46)

When the Son of Man comes in his glory, and all the angels with him, he will sit on his throne in heavenly glory. All the nations will be gathered before him, and he will separate the people one from another as a shepherd separates the sheep from the goats. He will put the sheep on his right and the goats on his left.

Then the King will say to those on his right, "Come, you who are blessed by my Father; take your inheritance, the kingdom prepared for you since the creation of the world. For I was hungry and you gave me something to eat, I was thirsty and you gave me something to drink, I was a stranger and you invited me in, I needed clothes and you clothed me, I was sick and you looked after me, I was in prison and you came to visit me."

Then the righteous will answer him, "Lord, when did we see you hungry and feed you, or thirsty and give you something to drink? When did we see you a stranger and invite you in, or needing clothes and clothe you? When did we see you sick or in prison and go to visit you?"

The King will reply, "I tell you the truth, whatever you did for one of the least of these brothers of mine, you did for me."

Then he will say to those on his left, "Depart from me, you who are cursed, into the eternal fire prepared for the devil and his angels. For I was hungry and you gave me nothing to eat, I was thirsty and you gave me nothing to drink, I was a stranger and you did not invite me in, I needed clothes and you did not clothe me, I was sick and in prison and you did not look after me."

They also will answer, "Lord, when did we see you hungry or thirsty or a stranger or needing clothes or sick or in prison, and did not help you?"

He will reply, "I tell you the truth, whatever you did not do for one of the least of these, you did not do for me."

> Then they will go away to eternal punishment, but the righteous to eternal life.

In this parable, Jesus is giving a stern warning to those who neglect the needy. We should be asking ourselves the question, "When we see someone who is poor and needy, do we stop to help them, or do we walk on by?" We could make up a lot of excuses for passing them by, just like people make up a lot of excuses for passing God by. And that's just what we'd be doing. You see, when we neglect the needy, what we're really doing is turning our backs on God. The next time you see someone in need, watch to see what you do. If you pass them by, then may I suggest checking yourself into God's hospital and letting Him do a little heart surgery? Helping the needy is really a matter of the heart, and God specializes in replacing old callous hearts with new ones full of generosity, grace, and mercy.

FIFTEEN
Building Surfboards, the Slow Way

It was a cloudless day, and the sun was radiating over Wannawaheenee like a jewel as Marty and Gerard walked along the beach, sinking their toes into the soft, warm sand.

It was wave season, and surfers from across Booga Booga Land were in town to challenge the big breakers. Marty's eyes were riveted on the surfers as they swooped down from the crests, shot through the tunnels, and spun out in the troughs. He was imagining what it would be like when all of a sudden he had an idea. He looked up at Gerard. "Hey, 'Stilts,'" he said to his tall giraffe friend, "howsabout we give it a try?"

Moments later the big giraffe and the little monkey were on their way to the surfboard rental shop. They rented five surfboards: one for Marty, and four for Gerard. Marty grabbed his board, raced to the water, and paddled excitedly to the middle of the bay. He bobbed up and down waiting for just the right wave, as Gerard walked out and stood beside him. A beautiful, long rolling wave was coming in, and Marty watched as it began to break. He caught it, and off he went, gripping the edge of the board with his toes. He dove down the face of the wave and into the tunnel, then switch-kicked through the pipe and fired out the open end. Then, cutting back into the wave, he barrel-rolled over the crest and ended his run by kicking out onto the beach. He looked back at Gerard and shouted, "Come on, Gerard, let's see you beat that!"

Gerard hopped onto his surfboards and rose eighteen feet above the water. Along the beach he could see people, lots of people, and they all were looking at him. Gerard gave a little smile as he looked over his shoulder at the incoming waves. He was waiting for just the right wave, and moments later, he saw it. It was huge and it looked like a snow-capped mountain range as it rumbled into the bay. *Okay, it's showtime!* Gerard thought as he clenched his teeth and flexed his muscles. The wave caught his surfboards and Gerard was cast onto center stage. His boards were rooster-tailing, and the hair on his neck blew back as he rocketed down the steep face of the wave. Then the wave's crown began to break, forming a huge tunnel. Gerard swung his boards around and headed straight in, disappearing under the colossal crest. The crowd held its breath.

Was that the end of Gerard? Could any giraffe come out of that big crashing wave alive? Moments later, Gerard raced out of the tunnel, grinning from ear to ear. The crowd cheered, and Gerard took a moment to wave a hoof before coming to a stop right beside Marty.

"Wallakamally, Marty! That was fun! Let's do it again!"

For the rest of the afternoon, Marty and Gerard surfed. They were having so much fun that they didn't stop until the waves faded into dribbles later that evening. As they carried their boards back to the rental shop, Gerard turned around to take one last look at the bay. As he did, one of his boards clipped Marty on the side of the head, sending him sprawling into the sand.

"Sorry, Marty."

Marty staggered to his feet, shaking the sand from his ears. He looked up at Gerard. "You know, Gerard, I just had an idea."

"Does it have anything to do with that helmet we've been talking about?"

"Not at all, big guy. I was thinking we should start up a surfboard company."

Gerard thought about the idea. They both loved surfing, and with this job, taking an extended holiday would never be a problem. The next day they sold their hotels and restaurants, then began working on their latest venture, the Big Booga Board Company.

The first thing they needed was a design for their surfboards.

They decided to hire a professional, and after placing an ad in the local newspaper, they chose two people to interview. The first candidate was a quick whip named Rilly Fast.

"So, Mr. Fast," Gerard began. "What do you have in mind for a board design?"

"Well, sir," Rilly said, "I was thinking along the lines of a five-hundred-gigahertz model."

"Oookay," Gerard said. "And just how will surfers benefit from that kind of board, Rilly?"

"I make fast boards, sir, and this one will give surfers all the speed they need."

"Wait a nanosecond," Marty interrupted. "I don't know if we're on the same wavelength here. What did you do for your last job, Rilly?"

"I worked in a computer shop," Rilly responded.

"Well, Rilly, I sure hope you can get that job back, because we're not looking for your kind of 'surf' board."

Rilly looked puzzled. "You mean you want the hang-ten, aloha kind? Not the Internet kind?"

"That's right," Marty said, as he waved "aloha" to Rilly.

The next candidate was a good-natured fellow named Spice Baker.

"So, Spice," Gerard began, "what kind of recipe do you have in mind for your design?"

"Well, I think I can add flavor by using garlic."

Gerard looked at Marty, then returned his gaze back to Spice. *Good Gimbo!* he thought.

"Spice, what does garlic have to do with designing boards?"

"Boards?" Spice asked. "Didn't your ad say 'bread'?" Marty and Gerard referred Spice to one of their old restaurants, then showed him to the door.

After looking through the applications again, and conducting a few more unsuccessful interviews, Marty and Gerard decided they would just design the surfboards themselves—then hire professional craftsmen to build them.

When the design was finally finished, Marty and Gerard hired three tradesmen: Lightning Lapotski, Hurricane Zacommin, and Slow. The workers were given everything they needed to get started, including their own workspace.

Lightning and Hurricane got off to a fast start, and within one week each had five boards built. Unfortunately, Slow's mind wasn't in his workspace; it was in outer space, and he had no boards to show for his week's worth of "work."

By the end of the second week, Lightning and Hurricane had upped their production to ten boards each. Slow was improving, as he had now begun to arrange his tools.

During the third week, Lightning made twenty-five boards; Hurricane made twenty-five; and Slow . . . well, Slow was starting to come to work late, and when he finally got around to looking at the plans, it was quitting time.

After four weeks, Slow still had nothing built. Marty called Gerard over and said, "I think it's time for Slow to go. You know, Gerard, I think if Slow's name was longer than four letters, he wouldn't be able to spell it." Gerard agreed Slow wasn't firing on all cylinders, but he suggested they give him a little more time. "I'll go and see if he needs some help," Gerard said, "and if he doesn't have a board built by the end of next week, then we'll let him go."

Gerard went to see Slow the next day. Slow was holding the plans upside down, with a puzzled look on his face. When he turned them right side up, he still had the same puzzled look.

"These plans just don't make sense, Gerard."

Patiently, Gerard helped Slow to understand the plans, and within a week, Slow had built his first surfboard. Slow was so excited! He zoomed down to Monty's Malt and Milkshake Shop and celebrated all evening with banana splits and chocolate shakes.

"I think things are going to work out just fine," Gerard said as he and Marty walked back to their tent that night. They had a late-night wiener roast, then stretched out on their cots. With the stars twinkling in the night sky and the waves lapping softly against the shoreline, the big giraffe and the little monkey closed their eyes and quietly drifted off to sleep.

The Parable of the Unfruitful Fig Tree

(Luke 13:6-9)

A man had a fig tree, planted in his vineyard, and he went to look for fruit on it, but did not find any. So he said to the man who took care of the vineyard, "For three years now I've been coming to look for fruit on this fig tree and haven't found any. Cut it down! Why should it use up the soil?"

"Sir," the man replied, "leave it alone for one more year, and I'll dig around it and fertilize it. If it bears fruit next year, fine! If not, then cut it down."

In this parable, Jesus is saying that people who hear God's message of repentance should respond to it while they still have time. The fig tree without fruit represents a person who has heard the message of repentance but has chosen to not respond to it. The extra year for the fig tree to bear fruit represents God's patience—in essence, another chance for that person to repent. A cut-down fig tree represents death, the time when a person's chances to repent are over. The message of this parable is clear and simple: repent while you still have time, or perish.

SIXTEEN
The Boojee Noojee

The sun was high in the sky above Wannawaheenee, and the beaches were full of people enjoying another beautiful Booga Booga Land day. Marty and Gerard had staked out a section of the beach and were just getting ready to start a game of volleyball. They weren't playing with a real volleyball, because it had popped when Marty had used it for dart practice. Instead, they were using the next best thing: a coconut.

Gerard dug his hooves into the sand, then started the game off by giving the coconut a mighty thwack. The "ball" rocketed into the air and went so high that it disappeared. Marty looked up, and, seeing that he had a bit of time, he then bent down to tie his shoelaces. Unfortunately, the coconut didn't go quite as high as Marty had thought, and when he looked up again, the coconut was right above his head. SMACK! He caught it right between the peepers. That gave him an idea. "Gerard, I think we should go whale watching."

Oookay, Gerard thought, *he must have got hit real hard that time.*

Later that afternoon, Marty and Gerard went down to the Wannawaheenee Whale Watching Company. This company was run by Mr. Tay Kadeezee, a businessman from Booga who had a knack for raking in the bamolies. He had a policy: "If no whales you see, then the trip is on me." This policy was proving to be very popular among the tourists—so popular in fact, that Tay had recently doubled the size of his fleet, and he now had ten boats in the water.

When Tay saw Marty and Gerard, he seemed a bit puzzled. He looked at Gerard, then looked at his boat, then looked at Gerard again. "I don't think so, Mr. Giraffe," Tay said slowly. "I don't think you're going to be able to get on my boat."

Marty looked at Gerard. "You can do it, Gerard. Remember the time you got on that bus in Toosmallforme?"

Gerard's mind went back to the day he had hopped onto the bus headed for Booga. He now looked at the boat intently, then backed up fifty paces. The boat was filled with older folk, and they all gasped when they saw the big giraffe stampeding toward them. Just as Gerard was about to jump, Tay hollered out, "Okay, I'll let you on! Just let me reinforce the roof first, okay?" Tay added the necessary supports, and moments later the boat left the bay with Marty sitting excitedly inside and Gerard standing stoutly on the roof.

After just five minutes, Marty stood up and looked over the edge. "I don't see any whales yet, Mr. Kadeezee."

"Just be patient, Marty," Mr. Kadeezee said. Five minutes later, Marty ran to the other side of the boat. "I still don't see any whales, Mr. Kadeezee." Every five minutes thereafter, Marty ran from one side of the boat to the other. His behavior was annoying the passengers, and eventually Mr. Kadeezee had to strap Marty to his seat.

Hours later, as the boat neared its destination, Gerard shouted out, "Ahoy, Captain! Whales spotted on the port side!"

All of the old folks jumped out of their seats and hurried to the right side of the boat. The boat rocked, and Gerard almost fell into the water. Mr. Kadeezee reminded the passengers that the port side was on the left. Everyone then scurried to the left side of the boat, almost dumping Gerard again. The boat was soon in the middle of the whales, and people began feeding them with popcorn and old bologna sandwiches.

After an hour of whale watching, it was time to head back.

This was the moment Marty had been waiting for. He jumped up and ran to the front of the boat. "Mr. Kadeezee, can I drive the boat, please?"

Mr. Kadeezee looked at Marty indecisively, then said, "Well . . . okay, Marty, but only if you're really careful."

"I'll be a good driver, Mr. Kadeezee," Marty said as he grabbed the throttle, then pinned it wide open. The boat shot forward, hurling Gerard off the roof and into the water. No one noticed, though, as everyone was on the floor, cowering under their seats.

Tay was flung to the rear of the boat and was trying to make his way back to Marty, as the boat snaked through the water. As Gerard bobbed up and down, he called out, "Excuse me . . . somebody! There's a giraffe overboard here. Hellooo?" His calls fell on deaf ears, though, as the boat continued on and eventually disappeared. Gerard drifted along for two hours before his ears picked up a faint sound in the distance. His hopes of being rescued heightened as he recognized the sound. It was the engine drone of another whale-watching boat.

"Captain," someone said as they spotted Gerard, "there's a whale out there!"

The captain, knowing they were still a long way from the whales, picked up his binoculars. "That's not a whale, that's the legendary Boojee Noojee!" The Boojee Noojee was Booga Booga Land's fabled sea monster, and the captain raced back to Wannawaheenee to tell everyone the news, leaving Gerard floating in the water. *Oh well*, Gerard thought, *I'll just make the best of the situation*. He began practicing his sidestroke and backstroke, as he slowly made his way back to Wannawaheenee.

It didn't take long for word to spread that one of Tay's boats had spotted the Boojee Noojee. In the ensuing weeks, people came in droves to Wannawaheenee, and Tay's business skyrocketed. He soon had fifty boats in the water.

At about that time, Tay began to think about his success. *Things are going extremely well*, he thought. *Maybe I should sell my business right now. That way I'll be rich, and I won't ever have to work again*. So, a short time later, Tay sold his whale-watching business and retired.

On the day of his retirement, Tay packed his fishing gear and headed out to a spot next to the whales. *Ahh, this is the life*, Tay thought as he dropped the boat's anchor, then sat back to relax.

Unfortunately, his anchor hit a whale on the head, and that was not a good thing. The whale became angry and swam madly through the water, heading toward Tay's boat. The monster fish torpedoed his boat, destroyed it, and left Tay floundering in the water. "Help me!" Tay cried, as the current started carrying him toward Losta Sola.

As the weeks passed with no word from Tay, his bank decided to take his money and divide it into two funds. The first was the "Find the Tay Fund," and the second was the "Find the Boojee Noojee Fund." Unfortunately, both funds soon ran out of money, and the searches were called off.

As Marty listened to his radio, he heard the news of the abandoned searches. "Gerard, do you think we should start looking for the Boojee Noojee and for Tay?"

"Marty, I have a feeling Tay is in a place where we don't want to go. And as for the Boojee Noojee, well, the most likely place to find it is in Snooza Snooza Land."

The Parable of the Rich Fool

(Luke 12:16-21)

The ground of a certain rich man produced a good crop. He thought to himself, "What shall I do? I have no place to store my crops."

Then he said, "This is what I'll do. I will tear down my barns and build bigger ones, and there I will store all my grain and my goods. And I'll say to myself, 'You have plenty of good things laid up for many years. Take life easy; eat, drink and be merry.'"

But God said to him, "You fool! This very night your life will be demanded from you. Then who will get what you have prepared for yourself?"

This is how it will be with anyone who stores up things for himself but is not rich toward God.

In this parable, Jesus is saying that material wealth is far less important than a relationship with God. People who have no regard for God and think that they are in control of their lives need to realize something: it's God who is in control of everything. The rich man, like Tay Kadeezee, was bent on storing up things for himself, thinking he was in control of his future when really he wasn't. God was.

People who live for money—and maybe even have so much that they could jump into it from a barn roof . . . and land safely—are the real losers in the end. Even if they live to enjoy their wealth here on earth, what good will it do them when they die? It will do them no good.

And what about their souls? Well, they will lose them, just like they lost their money. So live for God. You may find yourself lacking in earthly stuff, but you'll be jumping off the biggest of barn roofs when you get to heaven!

SEVENTEEN
The Boofabobs Face Extermination

It was a wonderful morning in Wannawaheenee, as Marty and Gerard sat down in the warm sunshine and prepared to eat breakfast. Marty poured himself some cereal, and was just about to stick his spoon in when a fly climbed into his bowl and began swimming. "Excuse me, the pool is closed," Marty said as he picked up the fly and cast it off. The soggy fly landed on the newspaper Gerard was reading. "Marty, could you hand me the fly swatter, please?" The fly took off and, like a stunt pilot in an air show, began performing acrobatics to avoid being hit by the swatter. As Gerard was flailing away at the fly, he accidentally hit Marty on the head.

"Oops. Sorry, Marty."

Marty lifted his head out of his cereal bowl and shook off some soggy Coconut Crispies. "Gerard, I could have drowned in there." Marty wiped some more Coconut Crispies off of his nose, then said, "Look, I have an idea."

"I know. You want scuba gear when you eat breakfast, right?"

"No . . . I was thinking we should go into the pest extermination business."

Gerard thought about the idea. The more he thought about it, the more he liked it. It just might be fun! The next day they sold their surfboard company and opened up the Big Booga Bug Blasting Company. The paint on their sign was barely dry when their first call came in. Marty answered the phone.

"Hello, Big Booga Bug Blasting. Marty speaking."

"Hello, Marty. This is Zander calling from the zoo. I was wondering if you could remove a pest from our premises?"

"No problem, Zander. What kind of pest is it? An ant? A termite? A flea?"

"It's a cat."

"Would that be 'cat' as in caterpillar, or 'cat' as in 'meow meow'?"

"It's the 'meow meow' kind, about the size of a leopard."

"It wouldn't happen to be a leopard, would it?" Marty asked.

"Well . . ."

"Sorry, Zander, we don't do leopards, but I know of a dog that might be interested." Marty gave Zander Rufus's phone number.

A short while later, Marty's phone rang again. This time it was a cricket who was having a few problems with some people. As Marty was talking to the cricket, another call came in.

"Hang on a minute, Mr. Cricket. I have a call on line two." On line two were some people who were having problems with a certain cricket. "I'll be right over," Marty said, as he hung up line two and went back to line one. "Uh, Mr. Cricket, stay where you are, we're coming right over." Marty and Gerard quickly packed up some supplies, then headed to the house where the problem cricket was reported.

When they arrived, Marty cautiously approached the house. "I think I hear the cricket inside," Marty said as he rushed out of the house and fired two canisters of Smoke-Em-Out gas through an open window.

"Marty, I'm not so sure that was a good idea," Gerard said.

Moments later, the occupants of the house came staggering out.

"The cricket's not in the house. It's in the shed," they gasped.

"Sorry about that," Marty said as he headed toward the shed.

When Marty arrived at the shed, he could see that the cricket had made itself right at home. It had its name on the door and even had its own mailbox. "I think I'll personally deliver a parcel," Marty said as he pulled out a Woocheewoochee rod, then set it outside of the cricket's door. He knocked on the door, then scampered away. When the cricket opened the door, he scratched his head and looked around. "Hmm, that's funny." Just then the Woocheewoochee rod exploded. KAPOWEE!! The cricket rocketed into the air and landed in Wannawaheenee Bay. "Okay, that's *not* funny," the woozy cricket chirped, as it was compacted by a surfboard then run over by a tour boat. With the job being done, Marty and Gerard returned to their office.

Shortly after returning, they received a visit from a couple of old acquaintances: Stan and his bandaged-up dog, Rufus.

"I see you took on that job for Zander," Marty said as he looked at Rufus. Rufus barked a weak "Woof," dog talk for "No more leopards, okay, Marty?"

Stan turned to Gerard and explained their reason for coming.

Their salmon farm had been taken over by a bunch of Boofabob bugs.

"And just how has your salmon farm been doing, Stan?" Gerard asked as he and Marty prepared to head out.

"Well, last year we planted sixty cans, and nothing grew."

Gerard looked at Marty . . . Marty looked at Rufus . . . Rufus looked at Stan . . . Stan looked at Marty and Gerard. "It wasn't my idea, okay? I was thinking of planting pickled herring," Stan said.

When Marty and Gerard arrived at the farm, they were quite surprised to see the extent of the Boofabob's occupation. The bugs had troops nestled in bunkers surrounding the farmhouse and scouts with binoculars on the roof. Gerard took a good look around, then said, "This one's going to take a little more than just a fumigation can, Marty. I think we're going to have to blast."

Gerard pulled out his custom cordless Holtmeister rock-coring drill and began drilling holes around the farmyard, while Marty filled the holes with a super blend of Kapowee rods. The Boofabobs looked on curiously, wondering what kind of crop Marty and Gerard were planting. When the holes were finally completed, Gerard announced, "It's showtime!" Marty took a front-row seat and waited for Gerard to detonate the blast.

KAPOWSKI!!! The blast rocked the countryside and blew the bugs beyond Booga Booga Land's atmosphere. As the bugs reentered the atmosphere, sparkles of light and small puffs of smoke filled the sky.

"Well, Marty, that should do it. Marty?" Gerard looked around, but Marty was nowhere to be seen.

The blast had sent not only the bugs high into the sky but Marty, too, and he was now miles away, sitting in a ditch. He realized he was in a wee bit of trouble when he tried to get up and discovered he couldn't move. Marty had landed on his feet, and that was something he wasn't used to. After a few hours of wondering what to do, he heard a car speedily approaching. "Phew," Marty sighed as he propped himself up. "I thought I'd be here all day."

The driver took a quick look at Marty, then sped by without stopping. "Then again, I just might be." Marty caught a glimpse of the car's rear license plate. It read, "Rilly Fast."

"I probably should have hired him to design those surfboards," Marty reflected.

A few minutes later a piece of scrap metal on wheels came sputtering by. It was Slam Pickens. "Hey, Slam!" Marty shouted out. "Slam, do you remember me?" Slam looked over at Marty, then kept on going.

Looks like he remembers. Probably hasn't gotten over that window-washing incident, Marty thought.

Just before sunset, Marty heard the bark of a dog. His hopes of being rescued were renewed, until he realized the bark belonged to Rufus. *He'd be the last one to stop and help me*, Marty thought. *I guess I shouldn't have played all of those pranks on him*. To Marty's surprise, Rufus stopped. He barked a cheerful "Woof," dog talk for "I'll help you, my little friend."

Friend? Marty thought. *After all I've done to him?*

Rufus put Marty on his back, then like a horse and cowboy they headed off into the sunset. Rufus took Marty to the Wannawaheenee hospital, bought him ice cream and bananas, then left, promising to return later for a visit.

Gerard came to the hospital a few hours later. As they talked about the events of the day, Marty commented, "You know, Gerard, that Rufus sure is a nice dog." They talked and talked, and when visiting hours were finally over, Gerard pulled his head out of the window and curled up on the front lawn of the hospital.

Marty looked out the window and thought, *I'm sure glad I have friends who care about me.* He then pulled the covers up over his head, and, in the twinkle of a star, he was sound asleep.

The Parable of the Good Samaritan
(Luke 10:30-37)

"A man was going down from Jerusalem to Jericho, when he fell into the hands of robbers. They stripped him of his clothes, beat him and went away, leaving him half dead. A priest happened to be going down the same road, and when he saw the man, he passed by on the other side. So too, a Levite, when he came to the place and saw him, passed by on the other side. But a Samaritan, as he traveled, came where the man was; and when he saw him, he took pity on him. He went to him and bandaged his wounds, pouring on oil and wine.

"Then he put the man on his own donkey, took him to an inn and took care of him. The next day he took out two silver coins and gave them to the innkeeper. 'Look after him,' he said, 'and when I return, I will reimburse you for any extra expense you may have.'

"Which of these three do you think was a neighbor to the man who fell into the hands of robbers?"

The expert in the law replied, "The one who had mercy on him."

Jesus told him, "Go and do likewise."

In this parable, Jesus is saying that we should show kindness to everyone, regardless of who they are or what situation they're in. The question really is, "Do you have a heart to help others?" If you came across someone who landed in a ditch, just as Marty did in our story, do you think you'd help them? Would you help them if it were someone you didn't like, or if it were someone who had been mean to you?

Would you help them if they had a different skin color or were richer or poorer than yourself? The next time you see someone in need, look beyond these things and imagine it's you in their situation. Then do for them what you would want them to do for you.

EIGHTEEN
Slam Pickens
Moves to Booga

It was early in the morning—too early for giraffes to be up, but not too early for monkeys. That would explain why Marty was already out of his sleeping bag and hopping around the tent. He entertained himself with a short game of "Jump Over the Sleeping Giraffe" before scooting over to the tent door. When he pulled back the flap and peeked outside, he could hardly believe his eyes.

"Hey, Gerard! Gerard! It's raining!"

Gerard woke up and looked drowsily over at Marty as the happy monkey grabbed a towel and a bottle of shampoo then ran outside. Gerard mumbled a little "Mmff," then rolled over in his sleeping bag and fell back to sleep. Marty poured the whole bottle of shampoo on his furry coat. Then he lathered up until he looked like a giant snowball. He ran back into the tent.

"Hey, Gerard, look. I'm the abominable snowman!"

Gerard woke up, looked at Marty, then sighed and went back to sleep.

I guess he's seen an abominable snowman before, Marty thought as he ran back outside. A few minutes later, the abominable snowman melted back into a monkey, and Marty grabbed his towel to dry off. He had left it in the rain, and it was soaked.

This isn't working, he thought as he poked his head back into the tent looking for Gerard's towel. He spotted the big rug underneath the sleeping giraffe and began tugging at it. Unfortunately, during one of his heaves, he lost his grip and went flying out the door.

His flight was stopped abruptly by a coconut tree, which he hit head first. If that weren't enough, a coconut came loose and dropped down, giving Marty a second bump on the head. One of those jolts gave him an idea. He walked back inside and said, "Gerard, I think we should go into the moving business." Gerard rolled over and thought about the idea.

"Okay, Marty," Gerard said sleepily. "We'll start first thing in the morning."

Realizing it was morning, Marty went over and started shaking the dozy giraffe until Gerard finally got out of his sleeping bag.

Gerard yawned and said, "Okay, Marty. Now what were you saying about cows?"

"Gerard, I didn't say anything about cows. I said we should go into the moving business." Marty explained his idea again, and this time Gerard heard every word. Marty finally persuaded Gerard to agree, and the next day they sold their extermination company and opened the doors of their new company, Moves by Marty and Gerard. They traded their dump truck in for a customized eighteen-foot-tall moving van, then decided that their first move would be their own. It was time to return to Booga.

After loading all of their possessions, they waved good-bye to the Wannawaheenians. Then Marty threw the big rig into first gear. The truck jerked and rocked as it pulled out of the parking lot, shaking Gerard like a rattle on a snake's tail. As Marty was chattering through the gears, he looked over at Gerard. Gerard was bracing himself nervously, pressing his hooves against the dashboard.

"Are you okay?" Marty asked.

"As long as you stay on the road, I'll be just fine," Gerard replied.

As they rumbled down the highway, motorists scattered to the left and right, stepping on the gas to avoid being hit by the titanic eighteen wheeler. Gerard was just starting to settle down when he noticed a roadside sign: Clearance: 16 Feet.

"Uh, Marty, do you see that overpass we're approaching?" Marty looked up just in time to duck. Gerard ducked too. But the truck didn't, and it came out the other side as a convertible.

"Hey, Gerard, check out the air conditioning," Marty said as he poked his head up through the roof. "Not bad, eh?" There was no reply, as Gerard was still shaking from the incident. When they finally arrived in Booga, Marty pulled up to their old house and locked on the air brakes. Their neighborhood had changed since they'd left, and many new homes and apartments now surrounded their old stomping grounds. It didn't take long for them to settle in, though, and in only a few days they were back in the business of moving.

One day as they were heading out on a long trip, they noticed an old putt-putt clunker of a car heading toward Booga. It was Slam Pickens. As they passed by, Marty blasted the truck's air horn. The blast knocked Slam's rear doors off, along with his back bumper. Slam kept puttering on, though, and eventually arrived in Booga, stopping in a puff of smoke outside of his new living quarters—a block and a half from Marty and Gerard's house.

A few days later, Marty and Gerard arrived home late at night. They were tired from their long haul, and they were just about to fall asleep when Slam's car pulled up. Putt putt, kaboom, clank! Moments later their doorbell rang. Marty looked over the edge of his bunk and said, "It's for you, Gerard." Gerard rolled out of bed and went to the door.

"Gerard," Slam said, "my brother Slim is coming to town tonight and I have no food. Can you spare me some feed?"

"Just a minute," Gerard said as he went to the kitchen. All he could find was some banana bread dough, leaves, and cold pizza.

He probably won't want the leaves, Gerard thought, and Marty's saving the pizza for breakfast. He went back to the door. "Sorry, Slam. All we have is banana bread dough."

"Do you think you could cook up a couple of loaves?"

"Uh, not right now, Slam. It's late, we're tired, and we need to get some sleep."

Slam left, and Gerard went back to bed. An hour later, they heard the familiar clanking car again and the ringing of their doorbell. Gerard looked up at Marty and said, "It's your turn this time."

Marty swung out of his bunk and over to the door.

"Slim called and said he's really hungry. He's arriving in half an hour. How many slices of pizza can you spare me?"

"You can't have any pizza, Slam."

"Well, what about banana bread then?"

"We're not baking banana bread tonight, do you understand? Now go away, we're trying to sleep."

Slam left and Marty climbed back into his bunk. An hour later, Slam's clunkster again pulled up to Marty and Gerard's house. This time Slam had to press the doorbell several times before they awoke. Marty looked at Gerard. "It's your turn, big guy."

"You get it, okay, Marty? I'm sleeping."

Slam kept hammering away at the doorbell until Marty finally got out of bed.

"Slim is here and he really wants a piece of pizza."

"Slam, do the words 'no pizza' sound familiar?"

"Well, can I have some banana bread then?"

"We don't have any banana bread."

"If you had baked it when I first came, you'd have some."

"Well, we didn't and we don't. Now look, we're trying to sleep. Come back in the morning, okay?"

"It is morning," Slam replied.

"Well, come back tomorrow morning then."

When Slam left, Marty disconnected the doorbell and went back to bed. An hour later, Slam's tin can on wheels pulled up to Marty and Gerard's place again. He took a few jabs at the doorbell, and then realized it was disconnected. He drove onto their front lawn and flashed his high beams into their bedroom window. When that didn't work, he climbed up and began banging on it. He still wasn't getting any response from inside, but he was starting to get some from the neighbors. They were now awake and shouting, "Give the guy some banana bread!"

Marty woke up. "Gerard, did you say something?"

When Gerard woke up, he heard the commotion outside and went to the window to investigate. The neighbors were marching toward their house. "Uh, Marty, I suddenly have this urge to bake banana bread."

An hour later, Slam was given four freshly cooked loaves.

"Thanks for your hospitality," Slam said as he headed off into the sunrise. With peace being restored to their neighborhood, Marty and Gerard dug into a couple of loaves themselves, then they packed their eighteen-wheeler with dreams and were on their way to Snooza Snooza Land.

The Parable of the Friend in Need

(Luke 11:5-8)

Suppose one of you has a friend, and he goes to him at midnight and says, "Friend, lend me three loaves of bread, because a friend of mine on a journey has come to me, and I have nothing to set before him."

Then the one inside answers, "Don't bother me. The door is already locked, and my children are with me in bed. I can't get up and give you anything." I tell you, though he will not get up and give him the bread because he is his friend, yet because of the man's boldness he will get up and give him as much as he needs.

In this parable, Jesus is talking about how we should come before God when we have a need. Just like the man came to his friend's house at midnight for bread, or like Slam kept hammering on Marty and Gerard's door for food, we, too, should be bold and persistent when we come before God. God honors persistence, and He meets the needs of those who seek Him diligently.

NINETEEN
The Runaway Dog

Fingers of sunlight streaked across Booga Booga Land as the sun peaked over the horizon to herald the coming of another glorious day. Marty was up early and standing on the front porch, eagerly awaiting the arrival of the ice-cream truck.

He waited and waited, but the truck didn't come. *Maybe they don't deliver this early in the morning*, Marty thought as he turned to go back inside. *I wonder if anyone does?* Marty quickly got his answer, as he was thwacked on the head by the morning newspaper. That gave him an idea. "Gerard, I think it's time to give Stan and Rufus a visit." As Gerard was thinking about Marty's idea, their doorbell rang. Marty answered it. "Rufus! What a pleasant surprise! I was just thinking about you!"

Rufus was carrying a backpack full of doggy biscuits, and he looked nervous. He barked a trite "Woof," dog talk for "I'm moving out, Marty, and I was wondering if I could cut a deal? My doggy biscuits for your moving van."

Marty thought about the offer. *Doggy biscuits . . . for our big, expensive truck. A few doggy biscuits in exchange for our livelihood.*

Marty thought hard, then replied, "It's a deal, Rufus. The truck's yours. Be careful, though. It jerks a lot when you throw it into first gear."

Rufus handed over the doggy biscuits, and then scrambled into the truck. With a quick wave, he pulled the big rig smoothly onto the street. *He's probably had a lot of experience with the farm tractor,* Marty thought as the eighteen-wheeler disappeared without a wobble. Marty hauled the doggy biscuits into the house. "Gerard, I just sold our truck for some doggy biscuits. What do you want me to do with them?" Gerard looked down at Marty. Marty looked up at Gerard. "Whaaat? It was Rufus's idea."

A few hours later their doorbell rang again. Marty went to the door. "Stan! Hey, Gerard, it's Stan! I hope you're not looking for a moving van, Stan."

"No, I'm looking for Rufus. This morning he asked for all of his doggy biscuits, then he disappeared. You haven't seen him, have you?"

Miles away, and rolling down the highway heading straight for Prodigal Park, was Rufus. *This is going to be such a blast,* he thought as he pulled his wheels up to the amusement park and slapped a For Sale sign on the door. It wasn't long before the truck was sold and Rufus was holding a fat wallet packed with bamolies. He entered the amusement park and looked around. *This is so . . . woah!* he thought, as the sights, smells, and sounds dazzled his senses. He rushed over to the nickel-diggers, then to the bumper cars, then to the mini-donut counter. *This is so much more fun than the farm! I'm never going back!*

Over the next few days, Rufus purchased his own doghouse and began making friends. At the park, he bought his friends hot dogs and rootiroo soda, and even paid for their rides. The bamolies flowed freely, and he was fast becoming the most popular pup in the park. Unfortunately, though, Rufus's wallet was getting thinner and thinner, and one day when he pulled it out, he discovered it was empty. He had spent all of his bamolies. For the first time, he was the one in need of help.

"Hey, Big-T," Rufus barked out to one of his friends, "can you spot me some coin for a rootiroo?" Big-T shook his head. "Sorry, Party-R, but this pup is penniless."

Just then a few of Rufus's other friends walked by, calling out, "Hey, Rufus, let's go ride the paddle boats."

"Okay," Rufus barked back. They all went over to the paddle pond and hopped into their boats, expecting Rufus to pay. "Hey, guys," Rufus barked out, "I'm out of bamolies. Could you foot my bill?" His "friends" got out of their boats and filed past Rufus. "We don't pay, we just play." For the first time Rufus felt lonely.

When he got home, things weren't getting any better. The bank was now threatening to foreclose on his doghouse.

In desperation, Rufus went back to Prodigal Park, this time looking for work, but no one would hire him. The next day the bank foreclosed on his doghouse, and Rufus was left on the street.

One night, tired and hungry, Rufus remembered the farm. "I wonder if Stan would take me back? Even his cats eat better than I do." He began practicing his "meow meows," hoping Stan would take him on as a cat. The next day he packed a few bare corn dog sticks and some old food wrappers, then headed for the farm.

He traveled for days, sleeping in ditches and drinking water from puddles. Occasionally, doubts would cross his mind. "What if Stan doesn't take me back? What if he doesn't even remember me?"

Each time Rufus somehow managed to erase those doubts and gathered enough energy to keep hobbling on.

Back on the farm, Stan had built a tall tower, and every day he had been climbing it to search the horizon for his lost dog. Marty and Gerard were helping too. Marty would sit on the barn roof with a telescope, and Gerard would stretch his full eighteen feet to scan land, sea, and sky.

One day, Stan jumped up and exclaimed, "I see Rufus!" Marty and Gerard looked into the distance and saw a little puff of dust.

"Are you sure, Stan?"

"It's Rufus I tell you!"

Stan jumped out of the tower, and in a whirlwind of dust he sped down the road toward Rufus. Marty jumped onto Gerard.

"Come on, big guy, let's go!" Gerard raced down the road, but he had a hard time keeping up with the accelerating Stan, who was now using every ounce of energy his body could muster as he literally ripped up the road.

As Stan approached Rufus, he dropped to his knees and came sliding to a stop. He threw his arms around Rufus and hugged him. "Welcome back, boy!"

Rufus was touched and whimpered a tearful "Woof," dog talk for "I don't deserve to be your dog anymore, Stan. Will you take me on as a cat?"

"Cat, shmat. I'll have none of that," Stan protested.

That night Stan threw a big party. His farm was full of friends, neighbors, and relatives who came to celebrate Rufus's homecoming. The choicest salmon was served, along with crispy leaf salad and thick coconut cream pie. As the party raged on into the night, Stan's hired hand, Crank, came in from the field. He poked his head in the door, and with a sour look on his face he asked, "What's all the commotion about?" Stan came over and explained, "Rufus is back!" Crank's face turned even more bitter.

Marty looked at Gerard. "Wow, he looks pretty crabby. If his face was any longer, I think we could run the quarter mile on it."

Crank went outside and pouted. He certainly wasn't going to celebrate the return of a wayward dog. Stan went out to try and console him, but it was of no use.

The party was still raging when Marty and Gerard left for home. When they arrived, they were so tired they just flopped into their bunks. "The party is now moving to Snooza Snooza Land," Marty said sleepily, as he yawned and plunked his head onto his pillow. They pulled their covers up over their heads, and in the shake of a dog's tail they were sound asleep.

The Parable of the Prodigal Son
(Luke 15:11-32)

There was a man who had two sons. The younger one said to his father, "Father, give me my share of the estate." So he divided his property between them.

Not long after that, the younger son got together all he had, set off for a distant country and there squandered his wealth in wild living. After he had spent everything, there was a severe famine in that whole country, and he began to be in need. So he went and hired himself out to a citizen of that country, who sent him to his fields to feed pigs. He longed to fill his stomach with the pods that the pigs were eating, but no one gave him anything.

When he came to his senses, he said, "How many of my father's hired men have food to spare, and here I am starving to death! I will set out and go back to my father and say to him: Father, I have sinned against heaven and against you. I am no longer worthy to be called your son; make me like one of your hired men." So he got up and went to his father.

But while he was still a long way off, his father saw him and was filled with compassion for him; he ran to his son, threw his arms around him and kissed him.

The son said to him, "Father, I have sinned against heaven and against you. I am no longer worthy to be called your son."

But the father said to his servants, "Quick! Bring the best robe and put it on him. Put a ring on his finger and sandals on his feet. Bring the fattened calf and kill it.

"Let's have a feast and celebrate. For this son of mine was dead and is alive again; he was lost and is found." So they began to celebrate.

Meanwhile, the older son was in the field. When he came near the house, he heard music and dancing. So he called one of the servants and asked him what was going on. "Your brother has come," he replied, "and your father has killed the fattened calf because he has him back safe and sound."

The older brother became angry and refused to go in. So his father went out and pleaded with him. But he answered his father, "Look! All these years I've been slaving for you and never disobeyed your orders. Yet you never gave me even a young goat so I could celebrate with my friends. But when this son of yours who has squandered your property with prostitutes comes home, you kill the fattened calf for him!"

"My son," the father said, "you are always with me, and everything I have is yours. But we had to celebrate and be glad, because this brother of yours was dead and is alive again; he was lost and is found."

The message of this parable is that God has an enduring love for His children, even when they disown Him. The younger son who left his father and all the riches of home is a picture of someone who once lived for God then went astray. The important point is that even though the son left his father, his father's love for him did not diminish. That's the same way God views His children. So if you once were living for God and now find yourself straying from Him, then you need to know this. You can still return to Him. He doesn't love you any less now than when you left Him. If you repent and return, He'll drop to His knees to welcome you back. So come on now, pack up your bags, and come on home. God's waiting for you with open arms.

TWENTY
Cows in the Courtroom

It was autumn in Booga Booga Land, and the leaves were just beginning to fall from the coconut trees. Marty was in the backyard doing some cleaning when Gerard poked his head out of the side door. "Marty, have you seen the vacuum cleaner?"

"Which one?" Marty called back from behind the house.

"The one I just bought for cleaning the carpets."

"Oh, that one."

"Well . . . ?"

"Gerard, have you ever wondered if you could use a vacuum cleaner to pick up leaves?"

Gerard peeked his head around the side of the house and yelled out, "Marty! My vacuum cleaner!" Gerard put a hoof over his brow, then took a deep breath and walked back into the house.

Hmm, Marty thought. *He never even mentioned how clean the lawn looked.*

Marty got back to work and began unclogging the vacuum cleaner, which had become plugged with leaves. He was sitting underneath their coconut tree, and he banged the vacuum cleaner against the tree. That loosened the last of the leaves on the tree, but, unfortunately, it also loosened a coconut. The coconut spiraled down, and when Marty looked up, he caught the coconut right between the peepers. He rubbed his head, and then wobbled into the house. "Gerard, I have an idea. I was thinking we should become Supreme Court judges."

Gerard wasn't even going to ask where that idea came from. "Marty, judges have to study law and be able to make wise decisions."

Marty thought for a moment, then said, "I can study law. Law is in my family. In fact, I have a brother-in-law *and* a sister-in-law." Gerard sighed, then made the decision, wise or not, to enroll in law school with Marty.

In their first semester, they both hit the books hard. Gerard hit the books academically, and Marty hit the books in the more literal sense, using a wooden gavel. Everywhere Marty went, he carried his little wooden hammer. He used it in the cafeteria. "Order in the cafeteria," he'd say as he pounded the countertop to get his hamburger.

He used it in the classroom too. "All rise, class is now in session," he'd say as he thumped the hammer on his desk when the professor walked in. Law school was proving to be quite fun for Marty.

Months passed. The months turned into years, and the years eventually turned into graduation day. Gerard's persistence was rewarded with a doctor of law degree, and Marty was given a golden gavel—the school's way of saying, "Thanks for attending our school, Marty. We'll miss you."

They began judging in the lower courts of the land and gradually worked their way up through the system. The eighteen-foot-tall giraffe sat behind the bench, while the little monkey sat beside him, with gavel in hand. They worked great as a team, and it came as no surprise when one day they were appointed as judges to the Supreme Court.

Their first case dealt with a dispute that had arisen out of a soccer game. The controversy began when two of the land's leading teams were in a showdown for supremacy. In the dying seconds of that match and with the score tied, a player from the Booga Blazer squad had broken free with the ball. He had a clear shot on net and booted the ball for what was sure to be the winning goal. Unfortunately, the ball ripped open and stuck to his foot. The game went to a shoot-out, and the Booga Blazers lost. The quality of the leather used for the ball came into question, and not knowing who supplied the leather, the soccer league launched a lawsuit against the only two leather suppliers in the land: Mr. Al Waizright and Mr. Ree Morse.

As people took their places in the courtroom, Marty pounded his gavel and announced, "Court is now in session." Mr. Al Waizright was the first to take the stand.

"Mr. Waizright," Gerard began, "the case before us is of great concern to the nation of Booga Booga Land. Supplying a substandard product to a national organization, in this case the National Soccer League, is a very serious offense. Mr. Waizright, I'd like to ask you where you get your leather from."

"Your Honor, my leather is the best in all of the land and only comes from genuine cows. In fact, my cows are raised in the north, where the toughest conditions prevail. The howling winds and the pouring hail make for the toughest hides around."

"Mr. Waizright, I'd like to see one of your cows, if you don't mind."

"Judge, I hope you're not hinting that I'm guilty. I'll have you know, I'm cleaner than an empty bean can in a rancher's camp."

"Be that as it may, Mr. Waizright, I'd still like to see that cow."

Court was adjourned, and a week later one of Mr. Waizright's cows made an appearance. Marty pounded the gavel. "Ouch!" He accidentally hit his thumb.

"Okay, Mr. Waizright," Gerard said, "I want proof that this cow is genuine."

"Oh, come on, Judge. What does it look like, a monkey?"

Marty banged the gavel again. "Ouch! Gerard, he's saying I look like that cow."

"Marty, we don't know if it's a cow yet. You can continue, Mr. Waizright."

"Judge, what do you want me to do, make it talk?"

"That sounds like a pretty good place to start, Mr. Waizright."

Al stuck two fingers in front of the cow, then asked, "How many fingers am I holding up?"

The cow slowly replied, "Moo, moo, moo."

"See, Judge, it's a cow. Maybe not a smart one, but it's a cow."

"Thank you, Mr. Waizright, I believe you have a genuine cow there. Do you have anything further to say before I hear Mr. Morse?"

"Yes, Your Honor. I think you're wasting your time trying to question me. I mean, I'm an ideal citizen—pretty close to perfect, I might add—and certainly not a weasel like Mr. Morse. Just look at him, Judge. I'm telling you, he's guilty!"

"That's enough, Mr. Waizright. Please have a seat. Mr. Morse, would you please come forward?" Mr. Morse approached the bench. "Mr. Morse, where do you get your cows from?"

"Your Honor, my cows come from the Deep South. They're a bit different than their northern kin, but they're just as hardy."

"May I see one please?"

"Yes sir, Your Honor. I have one right here." Mr. Morse brought his cow into the courtroom.

"That doesn't look like a cow, Mr. Morse."

"Well, that's just the way they grow down south, sir."

"Could I hear it talk please?"

"Well, I don't think it feels like talking right now, Your Honor."

"Mr. Morse, I need to hear your cow talk."

"Okay." Mr. Morse held up two fingers. The "cow" looked puzzled, then grunted, "Oink, oink."

"That doesn't sound like a cow, Mr. Morse. And why does it have such a flat nose?"

"Bad eyesight and a lot of trees, sir."

"Mr. Morse, I think your cow is a pig, and I find you guilty of supplying substandard leather to the National Soccer League."

"What did I tell you, Judge?" Al Waizright blurted out. "Throw the book at him!"

Ree Morse looked at the floor. "Your Honor, you're right. I am guilty and I apologize to all those I've offended, and I ask for their forgiveness." With his head still bowed, Ree Morse continued. "Your Honor, I know I deserve the dungeon." He started to cry. "But I want you to know, I really am sorry."

Gerard called Mr. Waizright back to the bench. With the two men standing before him, Gerard began, "Mr. Waizright, you are a very snobbish and haughty man, but you are free to go. Mr. Morse, I find your attitude of humility acceptable to this court. As Supreme Court judge of Booga Booga Land, I am granting you a full pardon. You also are free to go." The two men then left the courtroom.

With the long trial finally finished, Marty and Gerard went home and dug into a big dish of peppered poshkabba. After eating, they tucked themselves into their bunks, and Marty banged his gavel one last time. "Case closed," he said. "I'm adjourning for the night." With that, the little monkey magistrate and the tall giraffe judge quietly drifted off to Snooza Snooza Land.

The Parable of the Pharisee and the Tax Collector

(Luke 18:10-14)

Two men went up to the temple to pray, one a Pharisee and the other a tax collector. The Pharisee stood up and prayed about himself: "God, I thank you that I am not like other men—robbers, evildoers, adulterers—or even like this tax collector. I fast twice a week and give a tenth of all I get."

But the tax collector stood at a distance. He would not even look up to heaven, but beat his breast and said, "God, have mercy on me, a sinner."

I tell you that this man, rather than the other, went home justified before God. For everyone who exalts himself will be humbled, and he who humbles himself will be exalted.

In this parable, Jesus is saying that God does not want us to come before Him proudly, telling Him what good people we are. The Pharisee, who boasted about how good of a person he was and thought he was somehow better than others, did not impress God.

That kind of self-righteousness and arrogance was detestable, like biting into an apple and finding half of a worm. The tax collector, who came before God humbly and with a sincere heart, was the one who found favor. So when you come before God, come to Him humbly. He will hear you—and reward you by answering your heart's cry.

TWENTY-ONE
Conquering Mount Beepreepared

As he sat on the roof of his house with a batch of cookie dough, the sun's dazzling rays beamed down on Marty at the outset of another sweet summer day in Booga. Gerard was in the backyard fixing their lawn mower, which Marty had used to shred coconuts for his cookies. In the background Gerard could hear a steady thumping sound, and it seemed to be coming from the sidewalk. He looked up at Marty. Marty peeked over the edge of the roof and looked onto the sidewalk below. "How are those cookies looking, Gerard?" Gerard looked at the cookie dough Marty was tossing onto the sidewalk. "I don't know, Marty. I think they're kind of small and flat. Maybe you should come down and see for yourself."

Marty made a spectacle of his descent, flinging his hands into the air and jumping. Unfortunately, he caught his foot in the rain gutter and spun in a circle, walloping the wall face first. *If I didn't have a flat nose before, I've got one now*, Marty thought as he pried his foot loose and fell to the sidewalk below, hitting his head again. He looked up at Gerard. "Gerard, I have an idea."

"Would it have anything to do with removing rain gutters from houses?"

"No . . . I was thinking we should go climb a mountain."

The next day they resigned from their jobs as Supreme Court judges and began preparing for their mountaineering experience. They studied books and maps, then decided to challenge one of Booga Booga Land's premier peaks: Mount Beepreepared.

Marty jammed banana chips and pop into his backpack, then looked over at Gerard, who was loaded down with the mountain gear. "Marty, you wouldn't want to help me out by carrying a few of your things, would you?"

"Sorry, Gerard, my pack's full of food." Marty slung his little pack onto his back. "Come on. Let's go."

"Uh, Marty, I was wondering if maybe we should hire some guides for this trip?"

"Gerard, we're looking for a mountain here, not a flea on a football field. Good Gimbo!"

They headed into the bush without the guides, and after three days of wandering through the trees, they came to an opening. "This place looks awfully familiar," Marty said.

"You know, Marty, if it wasn't for Booga City Hall over there, and that house that looks exactly like ours, I'd say we'd be closing in on that mountain right about now." Marty got the hint. The next day they hired two teams of guides.

The first team was led by Ken Climb, and they were ready to go immediately. The other team was led by Billy Bungle, and they were still trying to figure out food supplies when the expedition left. "Oh well, I guess we'll just have to order up pizza," Billy said as his crew quickly flung their gunnysacks over their shoulders and headed into the bush behind Ken's competent crew. As the hike progressed, Billy's boys stumbled over rocks and roots, bumped into trees, and plopped into creeks and mud holes.

Ken and his crew were well in the lead when they encountered their first major obstacle: a deep, wide river. "Looks like we're going to need a suspension bridge," Ken said as he surveyed the situation. His crew quickly got to work, and the bridge was built before the others arrived. Ken's crew crossed, then continued on their way.

Billy's crew arrived minutes later. *This looks like fun*, Billy thought.

"Hank, you go first." Hank hopped onto the bridge and made it half-way across before falling into the water. "Hooty, you're next." Hooty hopped onto the bridge, and almost made it as far as Hank. "Now you, Jake." Jake jumped on the bridge and was bucked off after just three steps. "Do I have to show you guys how this is done?" Billy asked as he stepped onto the bridge and began swaggering across. About midway, he, too, fell in. The last member of Billy's team just decided to jump into the water and swim across.

Marty and Gerard were the last ones to arrive. Gerard took one look at the river, and then just walked across. Marty, on the other hand, hopped onto the bridge and began swinging from side to side. Four hours later, when he had finished playing on the bridge, they continued on their way.

After a few more days, Ken's crew came upon a deep canyon. Ken looked over the edge and into the abyss. "That sure is a deep one," he said as he pondered the problem. A few moments later he looked at his crew and said, "Okay, boys, we're going to bridge that gap. Pull out your chain saws!" As Ken and his crew were firing up their chain saws, Billy and his clan showed up. They took a look at the big timbers being cut down by Ken's crew, then decided to do some cutting of their own. They pulled out their chain saws and also began cutting, but the sticks and twigs they cut were so small that the only thing they were good for were toothpicks for mosquitoes.

After a few hours of cutting, the chain saws began running out of gas. Ken had brought extra fuel, but Billy's crew was bone dry. "Can we borrow some of your fuel?" Billy asked.

"Sorry, Bill, we may be needing it later on in the excursion. I suggest you go back to Booga or start cutting by hand."

Billy looked at his saw, then looked at the big trees. "I guess it's back to Booga, boys," Billy said as they packed their bags and began the long walk back.

As the hillbillies were rambling back, they bumped into Marty and Gerard. Just then Billy came up with an idea.

"You wouldn't happen to have a custom cordless Holtmeister rock-coring drill with you, would you, Gerard?"

"Well, I just might have," Gerard said as he sorted through his saddle pack. "What do you need it for?"

"We need to drill a gas well."

As Marty and Gerard continued on their way, Billy and his crew set up a drilling rig. They drilled for three days, first hitting regular gas, then premium, and—finally, what they were looking for—high octane. They filled their chain saws and headed back to the canyon.

Meanwhile, Ken's crew had constructed the bridge, and the gang there, including Marty and Gerard, had gone across. They waited for two days, then, with no sign of Billy or his crew, they decided to continue on. A short time after they left the bridge, a swarm of wood-eating Booga Lewkamakootis swooped down and ate it, so when Billy and his crew arrived, there was nothing left but a few wood chips. To add to Billy's problems, Ken and his crew had used up all of the big trees, and now there were no trees big enough to bridge the wide gap. As Billy sat down and looked across the deep canyon, he just shook his head. "I guess I'm what you'd call a Bungle in the jungle," he said, realizing they wouldn't be able to continue on.

On the other side, Marty, Gerard, and the rest of the climbers were approaching the peak of Mount Beepreepared, and soon they were at the top. "We made it, Gerard!" Marty shouted. They began celebrating by feasting on Banooki burgers, coconut cream pie, and rootiroo soda.

That night, as Marty and Gerard retired to their tent and tucked themselves into their cozy sleeping bags, Marty commented, "It's too bad Billy and his boys weren't prepared for the climb. They're missing out on something spectacular."

"They're missing out on the best, Marty," Gerard replied. Marty and Gerard then plunked their heads onto their pillows, and with a soft and gentle mountain breeze blowing in the background, the two contented climbers quietly drifted off to Snooza Snooza Land.

The Parable of the Ten Virgins

(Matthew 25:1-13)

At that time the kingdom of heaven will be like ten virgins who took their lamps and went out to meet the bridegroom. Five of them were foolish and five were wise. The foolish ones took their lamps but did not take any oil with them. The wise, however, took oil in jars along with their lamps. The bridegroom was a long time in coming and they all became drowsy and fell asleep.

At midnight the cry rang out: "Here's the bridegroom! Come out to meet him!"

Then all the virgins woke up and trimmed their lamps. The foolish ones said to the wise, "Give us some of your oil; our lamps are going out."

"No," they replied, "there may not be enough for both us and you. Instead, go to those who sell oil and buy some for yourselves."

But while they were on their way to buy the oil, the bridegroom arrived. The virgins who were ready went in with him to the wedding banquet. And the door was shut.

Later the others also came. "Sir! Sir!" they said. "Open the door for us!"

But he replied, "I tell you the truth, I don't know you."

Therefore keep watch, because you do not know the day or the hour.

This parable is talking about the second coming of Jesus. It asks this question: "Are you ready for His return?" Quite simply, if you're living for Him, then you're ready. If you're not living for Him, then you're not. Those who aren't ready will miss out on heaven, just like the five foolish virgins missed out on the banquet and like Billy Bungle and his crew missed out on climbing the mountain. The point of the parable is simply this: since no one knows when Jesus will return, make sure you're ready by living as if He were coming today.

TWENTY-TWO
The Amazing Gaboochi

Beams of sunlight shone through Marty and Gerard's kitchen window as they sat down for breakfast at the outset of another beautiful day in Booga. Gerard dug into his bowl of leaves, and when he was finished eating, he stood up and announced, "It's your turn to wash the dishes, Marty." Marty finished his cereal and took his empty coconut shell and Gerard's punch bowl over to the sink. "Gerard, could you throw your soup ladle over here, please?" Gerard threw his jumbo ladle over to Marty. Unfortunately, Marty had his back turned, and the ladle hit him on the head. That gave him an idea.

"Gerard, I think we should go into the inventing business."

Gerard thought about Marty's idea. *I've always wanted to become an inventor*, Gerard thought, *and Marty . . . well, if he bumps his head enough times, he'll come up with something.*

"Okay, Marty. Let's start inventing."

The next day Marty painted a sign for their new company, then showed it to Gerard. "So, what do you think, Gerard?"

"I think we can open up our new business as soon as you change that sign, Marty."

The sign read "Gadgets by Marty." The next day Marty repainted the sign, and "Gadgets by Marty *and* Gerard" opened for business.

Marty had the first brainwave. "Gerard, I think Booga Booga Land needs a rubber alarm clock." Marty was in the habit of throwing his alarm clock off of his bunk, and it was now so beat up that it looked like it had been the ball in a soccer match between two teams of wild horses—and it sounded like a cow in a pair of tight pajamas.

Gerard looked at Marty. "I'll tell you what, Marty. Why don't you work on that alarm clock idea of yours, and I'll take a look at a couple of other ideas, okay?"

Over the next several weeks, Marty and Gerard worked hard on their new inventions. Gerard had a full bag of ideas, and in those first few weeks he developed a car without wheels, a tree that barked at dogs, and an eighteen-foot telescopic straw. He was just thinking about his next invention when he looked over at Marty.

"How's that rubber alarm clock coming, Marty?"

"Well, it bounces okay, but it still sounds funny. What are you working on?"

"I'm trying to make a device that turns garbage into water. Got any ideas?" Marty set his alarm clock down and came over to Gerard. "You know Gerard, I think I might just know how to do it." Marty got right to work, and two days later he had a prototype ready for testing. "Gerard, I present to you, the amazin' Gaboochi. Throw in some garbage."

Gerard threw a load of kitchen scraps into one end of the machine, while Marty stood at the other end waiting to catch the water. Unfortunately, the Gaboochi didn't produce any water. It produced windows, cats, baseballs, and polychlorinated dibenzo p-dioxins—but no water. "Okay, so it needs a little tweaking," Marty said. "I'll have the problem fixed in a jiffy."

Three months later, and with a yard full of cats and baseballs, Marty decided to scrap the idea. He threw the Gaboochi into the trash can and went back to his rubber alarm clock.

The garbage was picked up later that day, and as the truck rumbled to the dump a strange thing happened. Water began to drip from the trash, and by the time the truck arrived at the dump, it was full of water.

Marty was dropping his alarm clock from his bunk when all of a sudden a thought crossed his mind. "Gerard, I think I know why the

Gaboochi didn't work. The reverse rivilsnocky switch was backward. We should have been throwing the Gaboochi into the garbage instead of throwing garbage into it!"

Marty raced out of the house toward the dump, with Gerard close behind. Smoke was pouring from their red-hot sneakers as they rounded the corners and sizzled down the streets. Trees shook, people's hats flew off, and traffic signs fluttered. They reached the dump just as the truck was unloading. Marty took a flying leap and reached out just in time to catch the Gaboochi. He sunk into the trash pile, and popped his head out a short time later. He had a big smile on his face as he held the Gaboochi high in the air. "It works, Gerard!"

They took the Gaboochi home, made a few adjustments, and then loaded it with garbage. This time a clear stream of water flowed out. They put the Gaboochi in their backyard and left it overnight to water their lawn.

The next morning when Marty looked out of the window, he saw two Gaboochis in their backyard. "Gerard, could you come over here for a second? There's something strange going on with those Gaboochis." Gerard came over and took a look.

"Woah, Marty! I wonder where that one came from?"

The next day when they saw four Gaboochis in their backyard, they were really confused. "Marty, I don't know where those things are coming from, but if this keeps up, we're going to be up to our kadoodles in Gaboochis." The next day, when eight Gaboochis showed up in their backyard, Marty and Gerard knew it was time to start selling them.

They opened up a store, and after selling only a few Gaboochis, they were swamped with requests for the amazing gadgets. Word of their new invention spread like wildfire, and within days, they could barely keep up with all of the requests. The Gaboochis sold like ice cubes in a desert, and soon Booga Booga Land was flooded with the little gizmos.

At that time, Marty and Gerard were hit by another big surprise. One day they looked into their backyard and there were no more Gaboochis. They just stopped showing up. It didn't take long for the news to spread, and within a few days the Gaboochi craze came to an end.

That wasn't the end for Marty and Gerard, though. Shortly thereafter, they received a call from President Bob. He was so impressed by their invention that he invited them to a special award ceremony. At the ceremony, amidst all the fluff and fanfare, Marty and Gerard were presented with the coveted Majorous Accomplishmentous Award, honoring outstanding Booga Booga Land inventors. Marty and Gerard responded humbly, "We really didn't do anything. The Gaboochis just kept on multiplying, and we still don't know how."

That night, after all the to-do and buzz of the award presentation, Marty and Gerard returned home to dine on a delicious dish of banana dobbinpopple. They then hopped into their bunks. Marty pulled out his rubber alarm clock and dropped it onto the floor. "Gerard, I'm sleeping in tomorrow. You can use my alarm clock so you wake up on time to make me breakfast."

"Marty, who said anything about . . ." But before Gerard could finish replying, the clock bounced off of the floor and hit him on the head, sending him into Snooza Snooza Land. *Hmm, I guess I'll be making my own breakfast,* the little monkey thought. He then tucked himself in, and, in the flash of a shooting star, he was sound asleep.

The Parable of the Growing Seed

(Mark 4:26-29)

This is what the kingdom of God is like. A man scatters seed on the ground. Night and day, whether he sleeps or gets up, the seed sprouts and grows, though he does not know how. All by itself the soil produces grain—first the stalk, then the head, then the full kernel in the head. As soon as the grain is ripe, he puts the sickle to it, because the harvest has come.

This parable is talking about how God's kingdom on earth grows. The seed represents God's Word, and the ground represents the world. So, just as the seed is scattered on the ground, God's Word goes out to the world, and just like seeds go through stages of growth, so does God's kingdom. The growth of God's kingdom depends on the response of people to God's Word. In places where many people accept God's Word and obey it, His kingdom grows quickly. In places where few people accept His Word, the growth is slower. At some point, God's kingdom on earth will come to an end, just like the Gaboochi craze came to an end. At that time, and nobody knows when it will be, Jesus will return to the earth to take His followers to heaven. That will be harvest time, a time of rewards for those who follow Jesus and a time of judgment for those who don't.

TWENTY-THREE
Gloryland

It was early in the morning, and both Marty and Gerard were still sound asleep. All of a sudden, a clash of thunder sounded, awakening Gerard. *That's odd*, he thought. *Thunder in the morning?* He went over to the window and looked outside. There wasn't a cloud in the sky. He then looked over at Marty. He was still sleeping. Just then another loud rumble sounded. Marty woke up and looked over at Gerard, thinking it was him snoring.

"It's not me," Gerard said. "It's coming from outside."

Marty climbed down from his bunk, went out the front door, and looked down the street. In the distance he could see a small cloud of smoke approaching, accompanied by a rackety rumble. *I recognize that sound*, Marty thought. *That's Slam Pickens's car.*

Marty stepped toward the street to get a closer look. Unfortunately, as the smoking rust bucket passed by, Slam's hood flew off and hit Marty on the head. That gave him an idea. He propped himself up, then staggered back into the house. "Gerard, I think we should buy Booga."

Gerard thought about the idea. "Well, why not?"

The next day Marty and Gerard bought the city of Booga. The first thing they did as the new owners was to make a few renovations. They started by installing rubber parking meters to prevent nose injuries to monkeys, then gave the Booga police force flashy new uniforms, and finally widened store aisles to accommodate tractors. After the renovations were complete, Marty and Gerard decided to take another holiday, this time on a cruise ship. They bought their own ship, then called up Slim, Slam, Stan, and Rufus and invited them to come along. They also hired a group of property managers to take care of Booga until they returned.

As the cruise ship pulled out of Booga Bay, the eclectic crew gave a hoot and a holler, and then they were on their way. Slim, Slam, Stan, and Rufus immediately headed for the swimming pool, while Marty and Gerard headed for the back deck. Gerard pulled out a book and sat down in a comfortable chair, while Marty pulled out his fishing gear and began trolling for whales, Booga Beluga whales.

Gerard was a few pages into his book when Marty felt a tug on his line. "Gerard, I think I've got one!" Marty began wrenching on his reel, heaving hard to haul in the mighty fish. Gerard looked over the top of his book at the struggling monkey. "Do you need any help, Marty?"

"I'm okay, Gerard. I've got the situation under total control."

Two minutes later, the exhausted monkey called Gerard over for some assistance. "That fish is huge, Gerard! You try hauling him in." Marty handed the rod over to Gerard, then went to rest on a cot. A few minutes later, Marty returned. "How's it going, Gerard?"

"I'm doing just fine, Marty," Gerard said as he nonchalantly spooled in the fish.

"You know, Gerard, I'm guessing that Beluga is thirty feet long, maybe forty. What if it's too big to fit on the boat?"

"I don't think you'll have to worry about that, Marty," Gerard said as he yanked the fish out of the water and onto the ship. It was a tiny sardine. Gerard looked down at Marty. Marty looked down at the little fish. "It was easy for you, Gerard. I was the one who made that whale burn off all the calories. That's why he shrunk!"

A few months later, and with no end in sight to their holiday, Marty and Gerard began to wonder how the property managers were doing back in Booga. They discussed the matter, then decided to send Slim and Slam to find out.

The cruise ship had several rocket-powered speedboats on board, and Slim and Slam eagerly hopped into one of them, then fired off to Booga. Upon their arrival, they discovered Booga had become a very unfriendly place. Restaurants and hotels would not let them in, and the property managers refused to meet with them.

What's more, when they returned to their boat, they discovered their engine was missing. It was a long trip back to the ship, as Slim and Slam paddled across the open sea. When Marty and Gerard heard what had happened, they were very unhappy. They decided to send Stan and Rufus to Booga, along with a letter asking the managers to apologize.

Rufus got into the boat and stood stoutly on the bow as Stan revved up the rocket engine. They gave a quick wave to Marty and Gerard, then were on their way. Two days later, the boat returned. Rufus had a bandage wrapped around his head, and Stan had a broken leg. "They beat us up," Stan said.

Marty and Gerard were now really upset. They turned their ship around and headed for Booga, prepared for battle.

As the cruise ship approached Booga Bay, Marty pulled out his binoculars. Then he exclaimed, "They've got cannons, Gerard!"

Marty turned on the ship's loudspeaker full blast and gave the command, "Give yourselves up, you slimy earthworms!"

"Uh, Marty," Gerard interrupted, "don't you think that's being a little too harsh?"

"Maybe you're right." Marty got on the loudspeaker again.

"Give yourselves up, you earthworms!"

Marty's plea was answered by a barrage of cannonfire.

"Maybe I should have left out the bit about the earthworms," Marty said as the ship was pelted by zucchini, bologna sandwiches, and tomatoes.

The ship returned fire with coconuts and bananas. Four hours later, with the ship's ammo getting dangerously low, Slam said to Slim, "I've got an idea." Slam fired up the rocket-powered speedboats and began sending them to shore. The crew aboard the ship watched as one after another the "torpedoes" hit their mark. The Booga cannons stopped firing, and there was silence.

"We got 'em!" Marty shouted. Moments later, the Booga cannons began firing again. "Okay, maybe not." The speedboats had knocked out some of the managers' firepower but had little effect on their overall forces. When Gerard realized the grave nature of the situation, he turned the ship around and headed back to sea.

The managers shouted and raised their hands in victory, thinking that was the last they'd see of Marty and Gerard. Gerard had other plans, though, as he set sail for Gloryland.

Upon arriving, he asked the king of Gloryland for a fleet of warships. The king sided with Gerard, and the next day an armada of ships headed for a showdown in Booga Bay. The ships began firing from miles away and relentlessly hammered the Booga managers. The ship's superior firepower was evident, as the managers responded with nothing more than a shower of cotton balls. The battle soon ended, and the managers were rounded up and carted onto the warships. As the armada left Booga Bay, the managers were loaded into the ships' cannons, then fired off to Losta Sola.

Marty and Gerard returned to Gloryland with the warships, where they were met by the king. "I heard Booga took a real beating," the king said. "Sorry about that, but now that you're here, I would like to show you something." The king took Marty and Gerard on a tour of Gloryland, showing them fields and forests, mountains and mansions. When they arrived at one of the grandest mansions in the land, the king stopped.

"Who lives there?" Marty asked.

"Have a look at the nameplate," the king said, as a smile came to his face. Marty and Gerard took a closer look at the nameplate. It had *their* names on it!

"It's yours," the king said.

Marty looked up at Gerard. Gerard looked down at Marty.

They both looked at the king. "Really?"

"Yes, really."

They were awestruck. Marty and Gerard ran down the long golden sidewalk, then stopped and ran back to the king. "For how long?"

"Forever," the king replied.

They looked at each other again, with eyes wide open. You never saw two bigger smiles as they thanked the king, then ran down the sidewalk to their new home. Their days of romping around Booga Booga Land were over, and, although those had been wonderful years, they were now on the edge of a bigger and better adventure. And what's more, it was an adventure that would last forever.

The Parable of the Tenants
(Luke 20:9-15)

A man planted a vineyard, rented it to some farmers and went away for a long time. At harvest time he sent a servant to the tenants so they would give him some of the fruit of the vineyard. But the tenants beat him and sent him away empty-handed. He sent another servant, but that one also they beat and treated shamefully and sent away empty-handed. He sent still a third, and they wounded him and threw him out.

Then the owner of the vineyard said, "What shall I do? I will send my son, whom I love; perhaps they will respect him."

But when the tenants saw him, they talked the matter over. "This is the heir," they said. "Let's kill him, and the inheritance will be ours." So they threw him out of the vineyard and killed him.

In this parable, Jesus is talking about a plan that God made a long time ago, and it includes you. His plan was to bring salvation to a world that was lost and sinful by sending His Son, Jesus, to earth. He used His messengers, the prophets, to let the world know that a Savior was on the way. Many people did not listen to God's prophets, though, and they treated them cruelly, just as the tenants mistreated the vineyard owner's servants. When God finally did send His Son to earth, the people killed Him. As bad as that sounds, something very good came out of it all. Jesus didn't stay dead. He rose again, and by conquering death He made a way for all of us to get to heaven. He died for the sins of the world, and if you put your trust in Him, you, too, can go to heaven.

And that's what this book is really all about: God's love and His provision for each one of us to one day be with Him in heaven. If you want to find out more about God's love for you, then pick up a Bible and start reading. From beginning to end, God's message is clear. He loves you. He wants you to put your trust in Him, and He wants to guide you through this life as your friend. No matter how old or how young you are, it's never too late or too early to turn to Him.

THE END

Stories inspired by the parables of Jesus, now in entertaining new DVD series!

Join Marty the Monkey and Gerard the Giraffe as they bungle their way through the paradise of Booga Booga Land, inadvertently learning lessons that Jesus taught many years ago. Each DVD includes 3 11-minute episodes in colorful, fast-paced animation. In these and many other adventures, the parables of Jesus are presented in a clear, challenging, and engaging way that the whole family will enjoy. Each DVD includes bonus features like coloring pages, trailers, and more.